나너의 기억   My Your Memory

나녀의 기억 My Your Memory

《나너의 기억》을 개최하며

윤범모
국립현대미술관 관장

그동안 참 많은 것들이 변해왔습니다. 1950년대 후반 컴퓨터의 발전과 함께 시작된 디지털 혁명은 본격적으로 우리의 일상을 바꿔놓기 시작했습니다. 이에 발맞춰 현대인은 원격으로 더 많은 일을 더 빨리 처리할 수 있게 되었습니다. 이는 경계를 허물면서 지구 반대편 세상과의 심리적 거리를 좁혀주었습니다. 하지만 최근 전 세계를 강타한 전염병으로 인해 대부분의 국가는 국경을 봉쇄했고, 물리적 접촉을 최소화하는 세상으로 바뀌었습니다.

디지털 문명은 변화된 일상에 빠르게 적응하며 직접 교류하지 않아도 일상생활이 가능하도록 다양한 방안을 제시하고 있습니다. 하지만 이러한 변화가 미래 세대에 어떻게 작용하게 될지 예측할 수 없습니다. 우리가 살았던 시대를 평가하는 것은 미래 세대의 몫입니다. 미래 세대가 현재 우리를 어떻게 기억하게 될지 알 수 없지만, 그들이 기억할 수 있는 정보를 남기는 것은 하나의 과제이기도 합니다.

국립현대미술관은 이러한 혼란과 격동의 시대에 과거, 현재, 미래를 관통하는 '기억'을 주제로 한 전시를 마련합니다. 《나너의 기억》은 '나너의 기억', '지금, 여기', '그때, 그곳' 세 개의 섹션으로 나뉘어 기획되었습니다. 각 섹션에서 소개하는 작품들을 통해 기억이란 무엇이고, 현재의 사회가 기억하는 것과 앞으로의 세대가 현재의 우리의 발자취를 더듬어 기억하게 될 것들에 대해 고민해보고자 합니다. 나아가 다양한 방식으로 재해석된 기억의 의미를 살펴보고, 미래의 공동체가 기억할 현재의 모습을 상상하며 우리 삶의 모습을 되돌아 볼 수 있는 기회가 되기를 바랍니다.

《나너의 기억》을 위해 귀한 작품을 출품해주신 국내외 작가 여러분을 비롯한 글래드스톤갤러리, 리만머핀, 마리안굿맨갤러리, 샹탈크루젤갤러리, 앤디워홀뮤지엄, 토마스데인갤러리, 파라다이스 아트스페이스 등 도움을 주신 기관 및 관계자 분들께 진심으로 감사의 말씀을 올립니다.

On *My Your Memory*

Youn Bummo
Director, National Museum of Modern and Contemporary Art, Korea

So many things have changed over the years. From its origins in the computer advancements of the late 1950s, the digital revolution has begun truly transforming our day-to-day lives. As a result, contemporary people are able to do more things faster by remote. It is a situation that has broken down boundaries, narrowing the psychological gap with the other side of the planet. Recently, however, the entire world has been struck by a pandemic that has changed everything, as most countries have moved to close their borders and minimize physical contact.

Digital civilization offers us various ways to adapt quickly to the altered state of events and continue living our lives without direct interactions. Yet we cannot foresee what new forms these changes might take on in future generations—for it is up to those generations to judge the times we are living in now. While we have no way of knowing how future generations will remember us, we face the task today of leaving behind information for them to remember us by.

During this time of confusion and turmoil, MMCA now presents an exhibition on a theme that runs through past, present, and future: memory. *My Your Memory* was organized with three sections: "My Your Memory," "Here and Now," and "That Time, That Place." Through the artwork presented in each section, the exhibition considers what memory is, what our society remembers today, and how future generations will remember us today as they retrace our footprints. Hopefully, it can also provide an opportunity to explore the meaning of remember as it is reinterpreted in different ways, while reflecting on community and our own lives as we imagine how we today might be remembered in the future.

I would like to offer my sincerest thanks to the Korean and overseas artists who are presenting their important work in *My Your Memory*, as well as the institutions and staff who provided their support, including Galerie Chantal Crousel, Gladstone Gallery, Lehmann Maupin, Marian Goodman Gallery, Paradise Art Space, The Andy Warhol Museum, and Thomas Dane Gallery.

나너의 기억

김은주

국립현대미술관 학예연구사

기억을 어떤 말로 설명할 수 있을까. 막연히 생각해보면, 기억은 과거에 대한 정보나 인상을 떠올려 서술하는 것 정도라고 말할 수 있지 않을까. 그런 서술 마저도 없다면 과거는 시간에 마모되어 사라져 버릴 불완전하고, 흐릿한 잔상뿐일 것이다. 뇌에서 자동적으로 실행되는 기억을 많은 분야에서 연구하고 있지만, 이에 대해 누군가 묻는다면 구체적으로 대답하는 것은 쉬운 일이 아니다. 하지만 반대로 그렇다는 것은 기억에 대해 아직 다양한 해석의 여지가 남아있다는 말이기도 할 터.

다양한 분야에서 오랫동안 기억이라는 미지의 세계를 탐구하려는 시도를 해왔다. 쉽게 떠올릴 수 있는 정신분석, 심리학, 철학 등의 분야뿐 아니라 최근에는 첨단 기술을 사용하여 그간 추측만 할 수 있었던 기억이라는 현상을 과학적으로 밝혀내고 있다. 그중 뇌 인지과학적 관점에서 기억의 메커니즘을 살펴보면, 기억은 일상의 수많은 정보를 잠재적으로 뇌에 저장했다가 정보의 중요도에 따라 취사선택하여 하나의 서사로 편집하는 것이라고 할 수 있다. 정보의 중요도는 개인의 가치관, 정체성, 문화 등 다양한 요소로 결정되며, 기억의 편집 과정에서 수면은 선택된 정보 간 공백을 좁히고, 기억의 서사를 좀 더 단단하게 다져주는 역할을 한다. 이렇게 우리의 기억은 정보의 저장과 망각의 과정을 거쳐 형성된 것이다.[1] 이외에도 기억으로 파생되는 다양한 과학적 현상이 활발히 연구되고 있다.

하지만 과학의 관점만으로는 서사, 분위기, 감정, 가치관, 정체성 등 공감각적이고 주관적인 해석을 포함하는 기억을 설명하기에 여전히 부족함이 있어 보인다. 우리가 일반적으로 기억하는 방식은 스스로 인지하지 못한 채 사건 당시의 수많은 비언어적 정보를 취합하여 하나의 장면으로 압축하는 것과 비슷하다. 이렇게 압축된 정보는 기억 저편으로 물러나 있다가 필요에 따라 상기된다. 예컨대 비극적인 사건의 피해자 대부분이 사건에 대한 기억을 진술할 때, 정확한 사실관계나 시간순에 의한 사실을 나열하는 것이 아니라 당시의 날씨, 분위기, 감정 같은 정보들을 뒤섞어 마치 토해내듯 입 밖으로 꺼내는 경우가 많다. 이는 사건에 대한 기억을 인과관계에 따라 간직하고 있던 것이 아니라 당시의 전체적인 상황을 머릿속에 압축해 두었다가 기억을 하나씩 꺼내고 있는 것이기 때문이다.

위에서 언급한 날씨, 분위기, 감정 등과 정보를 알라이다 아스만은 '정념'이라는 개념으로 설명한다. 그에 따르면 정념과 개인적인 삶의 기억이 만나면 하나의 불가분의 복합체가 된다. 이 둘의 관계는 의식적으로 형성되기도 하지만 때로는

[1]
전시 주제 관련 김민식 (연세대학교 심리학과 교수)과의 자문 내용 중에서 참고.

My Your Memory

Kim Eunju

Curator, National Museum of Modern and Contemporary Art, Korea

[1]
Referred to the consultation with Yonsei University psychology professor Kim Minsik concerning the exhibition topic.

How can we explain memory in words? Considered in vague terms, memory could be said to be something like the recollection and recounting of information or impressions concerning the past. Without that recounting, the past is nothing more than an incomplete, fuzzy afterimage, fated to be worn away by time. In various fields, there has been research on the workings of memory, which take place in the brain outside our recognition. But if asked about this, a given person would have a difficult time answering concretely. Conversely, this also means there is still room for different interpretations of memory.

For a long time, there have been efforts in different areas to explore the unknown world that is memory. Beyond the fields that come most readily to mind, such as psychoanalysis, psychology, and philosophy, recent years have seen the use of advanced technology to scientifically explicate the phenomenon of memory—something that we had hitherto only been able to speculate about. Examining the mechanism of memory through the lens of the cognitive neuroscience in particular, we could describe it as a matter of temporarily storing part of the vast volumes of information that we encounter from day to day, keeping it in our brain and selecting bits of it to edit into a narrative based on the information's importance. That information of importance is determined in turn by various elements such as individual values, identity, and culture; during the process of editing memories, sleep plays the role of closing the gaps in the selected information and cementing the narrative of memory into something more robust. In this way, our memories are formed through a process of storing and forgetting information.[1] There has also been prolific research into various other scientific phenomena derived from memory.

Yet it still appears that a scientific perspective alone is inadequate to explain memory, which encompasses synesthetic and subjective interpretations such as those associated with narrative, mood, emotion, values, and identity. Typically, our method of remembering is akin to unconsciously selecting from the vast amount of non-linguistic information at the time of an event and condensing it into a single scene. This condensed information recedes outside of memory, where it can be summoned again as needed. For instance, most victims of a tragedy who recount their memory of the incident do not simply state the precise facts or list off details in chronological order; often, they offer a mixture of other information from the time, including the weather and the overall atmosphere and emotions. This is because our memory of the incident is not something we harbor based on a cause-and-effect relationship; in our minds, we condense the overall situation at the time into memories that can be individually extracted.

Aleida Assmann explains the aforementioned information—such as weather,

극도로 자의적으로 결합되기 때문에 특정한 기억들 속에 들어있는 정념의 일부를 개개인이 조작할 수 없다. 그는 루소의 설명도 덧붙이는데, 이렇게 조작할 수 없음이 바로 루소가 정념을 기억의 가장 중요한 안정장치로 보는 요인이라는 것이다. 루소는 지나간 사실을 정확히 재구성할 수 없다는 것을 잘 알고 있었으므로 처음부터 자신의 기억이 객관적 진실성을 결여하고 있다고 보았다. 그러나 자신이 느끼는 정념만은 자신이 제어하거나 조작할 수 없으므로 진실하다고 주장했으며, 이 진실성이 '느낌의 사슬'(la chaîne des sentiments) 속에 고정되어 있다고 보았다.[2]

[2]
알라이다 아스만, 『기억의 공간: 문화적 기억의 형식과 변천』, 변학수, 채연숙 옮김(서울: 그린비, 2020), 340–346.

아스만과 루소의 설명처럼 정념은 개인의 기억 형성과 신빙성 입증에 영향을 미치지만, 특정 사건을 간접적으로 접하게 되는 비-체험자에게도 영향을 미친다. 우리는 과거에 일어난 모든 사건을 직접 경험할 수 없기에 학습을 통해 간접적으로 접하게 되는 경우가 많은데, 이때 이 '정념'에 대한 기록은 매체를 통한 간접 경험을 보다 풍성하게 자신의 기억으로 저장될 수 있도록 해준다. 우리가 역사를 객관적인 기록에 대한 학습이 아니라 보다 감정적이고 주관적인 관점에서 바라볼 수 있는 것도 정념이 작동했기 때문일 것이다.

이번 전시에서는 각 작가가 '기억'을 자신만의 조형언어로 해석한 작품을 소개한다. 이 작품들은 우리가 특정 사건을 어떻게 기억하고 있고, 무엇 때문에 기억하게 되었는지에 대한 주관적인 이야기를 담고 있으며, 객관적 사실 정보가 아니라 '정념'이라 표현되는 사건 당시의 느낌과 감정을 드러내는 방식으로 제작되었다. 전시 제목 《나너의 기억》은 사회 속에서 존재하는 개인의 기억은 타자와의 관계 속에서 형성되기 때문에 온전히 자신으로부터 형성된 것이 아니라 서로의 기억이 혼재되고, 중첩된다는 의미를 담고 있으며, 이것을 '나'와 '너'를 조사 없이 붙여 써 시각적으로 표현하고자 했다. 전시는 '나너의 기억', '지금, 여기' 그리고 '그때, 그곳' 이렇게 총 세 개의 섹션으로 나뉜다.

나너의 기억

'나너의 기억'에서는 기억 형성에 미치는 다양한 요소에 대해 살펴본다. 기억 형성에 영향을 미치는 요소를 찾고자 하면 너무나 많은 요소가 있겠지만, '나너의 기억'에서는 대표적으로 인간 뇌에서 일어나는 생리적 현상을 기반으로 발생하는 현상에서부터 사회에서 타인과 함께 살아가면서 일어나는 사건이 기억에 미치는 영향 등에 주목한다.

앞에서 설명했듯 우리는 일상에서 받아들인 정보를 수면을 통해 편집하고 하나의 서사로 구성하는데, 전시 도입부에서 소개되는 앤디 워홀의 〈수면〉(1963)은 그 과정을 은유적으로 보여준다. 워홀은 달러, 신발, 유명인, 식품 등 대중에게 친숙한 이미지를 작품에 활용하면서 자본주의와 대중매체로 대표되던 20세기 미국 문화를 표현한 세계적인 팝 아티스트다. 초기에는 경박한 이미지를 작품화했다는 혹평을 받기도 했으나 변함없는 예술세계를 보여주면서 미국 문화의 이면에 가려진 진부함과 공허함을 표현해냈다는 평을 받았고, 모더니즘이 만연했던 당시 미술계의 흐름을

[2]
Aleida Assmann, *Cultural Memory and Western Civilization*, trans. Byeon Haksu & Chae Yeonsuk (Seoul: Greenbee, 2020), 340–346.

atmosphere, and emotions—in terms of the concept of "sentiments." According to her, sentiments and the memories of individual life come together to form an inextricable complex. The relationship between the two may be shaped consciously, but it also combines in exceedingly arbitrary ways at times, so that individuals are not able to manipulate portions of the sentiments contained within certain memories. Assmann also includes the account of Jean-Jacques Rousseau, explaining that this non-manipulability is precisely the reason that Rousseau views sentiments as the most crucial safeguard of memory. Rousseau was well aware that past information cannot be reconstructed precisely, and he saw his own memories as lacking objective truthfulness from the outset. Yet he argued that only the sentiments he felt were true, since he could not control or manipulate them, and he viewed that truthfulness as being fixed within the "chain of sentiments" (*la chaîne des sentiments*).[2]

As Assmann and Rousseau explain, sentiments influence the formation of individual memories and proof of their credibility, but they also influence non-experiencers of particular events who encounter them only indirectly. Since we cannot experience all the events of the past ourselves, there are many of them that we encounter indirectly through learning, and this recording of "sentiments" allows us to store indirect media-based experiences more richly as our own memories. When we are able to view history not as the learning of objective records but as something from a more emotional and subjective standpoint, that may be because sentiments have come into play.

Each of the artists in this exhibition presents a work that interprets "memory" through their unique aesthetic language. The artworks include subjective stories about how we remember certain events and what has caused us to remember something. They are also produced in ways that show the feeling and emotion from the time of the event—what we refer to as "sentiments"—rather than objective, factual information. The exhibition title *My Your Memory* expresses the idea that because the memories of individuals within society are formed within relationships to others, their memories are not formed entirely from themselves but become intermingled and juxtaposed with those of other people. The exhibition consists of three sections: "My Your Memory," "Here and Now," and "That Time, That Place."

My Your Memory

In "My Your Memory", we examine the different elements that influence the formation of memories. If we go looking for the elements that affect our memory formation, we may find a great many—but in "My Your Memory", the representative focus is on phenomena based on physiological occurrences in the human brain, as well as the events that arise when we live together with others in society.

As explained earlier, the process of sleep allows us to shape the information we receive from our daily life into a narrative. Andy Warhol's *Sleep* (1963), which is presented at the start of the exhibition, shows that process metaphorically. A world-renowned pop artist, Warhol represented the 20th century American culture exemplified by capitalism and mass media, using images in his work that were familiar to the public: dollar bills, shoes, celebrities, food, and so forth. Early in his career, he was accused of producing artwork that consisted of shallow images. Yet by showing an unchanging artistic world, he was also seen as having expressed the hidden banality and emptiness on the other side of American culture, and at a time when modernism was rife in the art

팝아트로 이끄는 역할을 했다.

그의 작품 〈수면〉은 20세기 시의 거장 존 지오르노가 자는 모습을 5시간 21분 동안 촬영한 것이다. 이처럼 촬영 시간이 아주 길거나 짧은 기법은 1960년대 워홀이 전통적인 영화 기법에 도전하고자 실험했던 '안티필름'(anti films)의 일환이다. 워홀은 친구 존 지오르노가 자면서 무의식의 심연에 빠져 있는 모든 순간을 빠짐없이 찍기 위해 밤새 필름을 수백 통이나 갈아 끼워가며 영상에 담아냈다.

〈수면〉이 기억 형성 과정을 상징적으로 보여주었다면, 허만 콜겐의 〈망막〉(2018)은 기억이 뇌에서 어떤 작용을 통해 형성되는지를 보다 시각적으로 표현한다. 캐나다 몬트리올을 기반으로 활동하는 작가는 뉴미디어 작품을 꾸준히 선보이며 국제적인 명성을 얻고 있다. 그는 인간의 지각과 감각에 관심을 가지고 시각과 청각의 내밀한 관계성을 비디오, 퍼포먼스, 설치 등 다양한 매체의 속성을 교차시키면서 새로운 감각을 자극하는 방식으로 표현한다.

〈망막〉은 빛으로 전달되는 정보가 뇌 신경을 거쳐 기억으로 저장되는 과정을 시각적으로 보여주는 작품이다. 흐릿하고 파편적인 이미지와 빛이 뇌 신경을 관통하는 과정을 표현한 레이저 맵핑을 중첩시켜 뇌 속 어딘가에 자리 잡고 있을 기억에 대한 이미지를 상징적으로 표현했다. 자연계의 수많은 현상 중 인간이 지각할 수 있는 현상은 오감이 허락하는 범위 안에 제한되어 있다. 말하자면 우리는 시-감각이 허락하는 범위에서만 볼 수 있다. 따라서 보고 있는 대상에 대한 모든 자연계의 정보를 받아들이고 있다고 할 수 없는 것이다. 예컨대 인간은 지각할 수 없지만, 주변에 존재하는 초음파, 전자파, 적·자외선 등 같은 현상들을 생각해볼 수 있다. 작가는 인간의 지각적 한계에 대해 지적하고, 실재 현상과 우리가 그것을 지각하고 기억한 장면 간의 괴리를 이야기한다. 작품이 말하듯 정보가 빛의 형태로 뇌에 들어오는 과정에서 변형되고 왜곡되어 우리가 형성하는 기억에 영향을 미친다면 과연 이 기억의 객관성은 어디에서 찾아야 할까. 이 같은 일련의 질문은 인간의 기억은 태생적으로 주관적인 것이었으며, 우리가 '기억하고 있는 것'의 실체는 무엇인지에 대한 근본적인 질문을 던져볼 것을 제안하는 것이다.

반면 양정욱과 임윤경은 개인이 사회 속에서 타인과 상호 관계를 맺으며 형성하는 기억을 이야기한다. 양정욱은 주로 타인을 주변인의 시각에서 관찰하고, 타인의 삶을 자신의 방식대로 상상하여 작품의 서사를 구성해왔다. 그는 경비원, 병실의 노인, 종업원, 안마사 등 주변에서 흔히 찾아볼 수 있지만 쉽게 지나쳐버리는 사람들의 이야기에 주목한다. 2008년까지 회화 작업을 주로 하던 작가는 〈남희에게 주는 양태환 선수〉(2008)라는 작품 이후로 관찰한 대상의 서사가 녹아 있는 키네틱 조각 작품을 꾸준히 선보이고 있다.

〈피곤은 언제나 꿈과 함께〉(2013)는 작가가 젊었을 때 생계를 위해 편의점에서 아르바이트했던 당시를 회상하며 제작한 작품이다. 손님이 잘 들지 않는 편의점에서 새벽 근무를 하는 중 이 무료한 노동의 시간을 함께하고 있는 길 건너편의 경비원을 바라보며, 그의 이야기를 상상하여 작품으로 표현했다. 나무 조각들이 유기적으로

world, he played a role in steering it in the direction of Pop Art.

To produce his work *Sleep*, Warhol filmed the great 20th century poet John Giorno sleeping for five hours and twenty-one minutes. This technique involving both very long and very brief filming times was developed as part of an "anti-films" approach that Warhol experimented with during the 1960s as a challenge to traditional cinema. To film every moment of his friend Giorno deep within the abyss of unconsciousness, Warhol spent the entire night capturing him with his lens, replacing his film canisters hundreds of times in the process.

While *Sleep* illustrates the process of memory formation in a symbolic way, *RETINA* (2018) by Herman Kolgen offers a more visual representation of the processes through which memories form in the brain. Based in the Canadian city of Montréal, the artist has made a name for himself internationally with his New Media work. He is interested in human perception and senses, juxtaposing the properties of different media (including film, performance, and installation) and devising new methods of stimulating the senses in order to express the hidden relationship between sight and hearing.

RETINA is a work that visually presents the process of information transmitted as light as it passes through the brain's neurons to be stored as memory. By overlapping blurred and fragmentary images with laser mapping showing the process of light passing through neurons, Kolgen symbolically shares an image of how memories might exist somewhere within our brains. Of all the innumerable phenomena of the natural world, the kinds that humans are capable of perceiving are limited to the scope of what our senses allow. In a word, we can only see within the range of what our sense of vision permits. In that sense, we cannot be said to internalize all the natural information about the object we are viewing. As an example, we may think of the phenomena that exist around us but that humans cannot perceive, such as ultrasonic waves, electromagnetic waves, or infrared and ultraviolet light. Remarking on human perceptual limitations, the artist focuses on the gap between the actual phenomena and the image through which we perceive and remember it. If, as the work indicates, the memories that we form are influenced by alterations and distortions that arise as information enters the brain in the form of light, where might we discover the objectivity of memory? Through questions like these, the work presents human memory as something inherently subjective, suggesting that we might ask fundamental questions about the true nature of what we "remember."

In contrast, Yang Junguk and Lim Yoonkyung examine the memories formed through the individual's interactions with others in society. Yang mainly observes others from the perspective of someone on the periphery, imagining other people's lives in his own way to form the narrative of his work. He focuses on the stories of people we often see around us but easily overlook: security workers, elderly people in hospital rooms, service workers, massage therapists, and so forth. After working primarily in painting through 2008, Yang has been regularly producing kinetic (moving) sculptural work that incorporates the narratives of those he has observed—an approach that began with his work *Yang Taehwan Gives a Gift to Namhee* (2008).

Fatigue Always Comes with a Dream (2013) is a piece that the artist created as he recalled a time when he was younger and worked part-time at a convenience store to make ends meet. While working late at night at the store, which had few customers, he saw a security guard across the street who shared the same enervating working hours.

연결되어 제작된 작품은 동력에 의해 천천히 상하운동을 하면서 규칙적으로 페트병을 치며 소리를 낸다. 천천히 움직이는 조각은 새벽에 졸고 있는 경비원의 나른함을 느낄 수 있게 해주고, 페트병이 내는 소리는 그가 화들짝 놀라며 졸음에서 벗어나는 순간을 나타낸다.

이 작품은 타인이 기억을 생성하는 모습을 목격한 작가의 기억을 표현한다. 경비원이 졸면서 어떤 꿈을 꾸며 기억을 생성하고 있는지는 알 수 없지만, 바라보는 풍경 속 대상을 관찰하고 상상하며 자신의 기억을 형성하는 것은 작가의 개인적 선택이다. 자신과 타인의 기억이 생성되는 순간은 겹치더라도 각자 다른 정보를 받아들이기 때문에 서로 다른 기억을 간직하게 되는 것이다. 심지어 졸고 있는 경비원은 자신이 타인의 기억 속 어딘가에 존재하게 되리라고는 생각하지 못했을 것이다. 반면 당시 작가가 바라보던 경비원은 자신과 같이 삶의 고단함을 느끼고 있을 존재였으리라.

임윤경은 양정욱과 마찬가지로 사회 속 개인의 기억을 이야기하지만, 주변인의 관점으로 타인을 관찰하는 것이 아니라 적극적으로 타인과의 관계에 참여한다. 특히 특정 사회 속에서 개인이 관계를 맺으며 정체성을 형성해 가는 과정에서 드러나는 모순과 갈등에 주목한다. 작가는 개인이 사회에서 맺게 되는 다양한 형태의 관습화된 관계를 작가가 상정하는 방식으로 해체하고, 이를 재구성하는 과정을 통해 관계의 근본적인 문제점을 표면화하는 작업을 주로 선보여 왔다. 집단 내 개인의 사회적 위치, 관습이나 제도 같은 사회적 규범과 개인의 관계 맺음, 사적 영역과 공적 영역의 관계 설정 등과 같은 관심을 바탕으로 비디오, 사운드, 영상, 텍스트 등의 매체를 탐구한다.

〈Q&A〉(2016)는 작가가 어린 시절 집에 고용되었던 외국인 가사도우미를 모티브로 제작되었다. 두 참여자가 실제 서로 마주 보고 묻고 답하는 모습을 실시간 영상 촬영하고, 통역 과정을 편집하여 한 개의 영상을 두 개의 영상으로 분할한 뒤 재배치한 영상설치 작업이다. 작품에 등장하는 화자는 총 5명으로, 고용주였던 어머니(최인옥)와 그의 딸(임윤경), 고용인이었던 외국인 가사도우미, 그리고 다른 가정집의 외국인 가정부(쉴라)와 그의 딸(케이시)이다. 이들은 모두 같은 시점을 회상하며 서로에게 당시의 상황을 질문한다. 예컨대, 고용주였던 어머니(최인옥)가 다른 집 가정부의 딸(케이시)에게 타국으로 일하러 간 어머니와 떨어져 지냈던 시기의 심정을 질문하거나, 다른 집 가정부인(쉴라)이 고용주 딸(임윤경)에게 어린 시절 고용되었던 가정부와의 관계에 대해 질문하며 당시의 기억을 공유하는 것이다. 또, 임윤경의 집에서 일했던 외국인 가정부가 일을 그만두게 된 상황을 묘사하는 것과 그의 어머니(고용주)가 기억하는 것이 다른 것을 확인한다.

작가는 특정 사회나 관계 속에서 개인이 처한 상황, 정체성, 언어, 문화 등에 따라 기억이 다르게 형성될 수도 있다는 것을 작품으로 표현한다. 자유주의적인 근대적 개인의 이론을 확립한 존 로크에 따르면 기억은 인격동일성의 중심축으로서 개인의 정체성은 자신의 경험과 회상을 통해 근거 지어지는 정체성이며,[3] 반대로 이렇게 형성된 정체성은 앞으로의 경험과 기억에도 영향을 미치게 된다. 이 같은 로크의

[3]
김옥경, 「로크에서 기억과 근대적 개인의 자기정체성」, 『철학논집』, 제42집, 2015, 262~264.

He imagined the story of that guard, which he would eventually express in his artwork. Created from pieces of wood organically linked together, the work is moved slowly up and down by a motor, producing noises through the regular striking of plastic bottles. The slow movements of the sculpture convey a sense of the security guard's languor as he dozes off late at night, while the sounds coming from the plastic bottles evoke the moments where he is startled out of his slumber.

The work expresses Yang's memories of seeing another person forming memories. While there was no way for him to know what dreams the sleeping security guard was dreaming and what memories he was forming, the creation of his own memories as he observed and imagined an object with the landscape he viewed represents a personal choice. Even when the moments that our memories and other people's memories are formed happen to overlap, we are each receiving different information, which means that we acquire direct memories. The sleeping security guard surely had no idea that he would be present somewhere in someone else's memory. But to the observing Yang at the time, the security guard would have been someone sharing in the same sort of weary life.

Like Yang Junguk, Lim Yoonkyung also examines the memories of individuals within society. But rather than observing others from a peripheral perspective, she actively takes part in relationships with others. In particular, she focuses on the conflicts and contractions that arise as individuals form their identity amid their relationships in a particular society. She has chiefly presented artwork using methods introduced by the artist to deconstruct the various kinds of routine relationships that individuals form in society, while using the process of their reconstruction to bring to the surface fundamental issues in those relationships. She has also explored media such as film, sound, moving images, and text as part of her interest in topics such as the social status of individuals within groups; the ways in which individuals form relationships with conventions, institutions, and other social norms; and the ways relationships are established between the public and private spheres.

The motif for Lim's *Q&A* (2016) comes from a foreign housekeeper who was employed by the artist's family when she was a child. For this video installation work, she filmed a real-time video of two participants actually sitting face-to-face as they asked and answer questions; as the artist edited the interpretation process, she split the single video into two different videos and rearranged them. A total of five speakers appear in the work: the artist's mother (played by Choi Inok), who employed the housekeeper; her daughter (Lim herself); the foreign housekeeper; and another foreign housekeeper working for a different family (Sheila) and her daughter (Kaycee). The five of them recall the same moment in time and ask each other questions about the situation. For example, the mother asks the other family's housekeeper's daughter Kaycee how it felt to live apart from her mother while she was working overseas, while the other housekeeper (Sheila) asks the daughter (played by Lim) about her relationship with the housekeeper who worked for her family when she was a child. In the process, they share memories of the time. We also observe the difference between how the foreign housekeeper who worked for Lim's family characterizes her decision to quit the job and how Lim's mother (her employer) remembers it.

Through her artwork, the artist expresses how memories may be differently shaped according to the circumstances, identity, language, culture, and so forth of individuals

주장과 임윤경의 작품을 미루어 보아 정체성과 기억 형성은 밀접한 관계에 놓여있다고 볼 수 있고, 정체성을 결정짓는 다양한 사회적 요소 또한 상호 영향을 주고받는다고 할 수 있다.

'나너의 기억'에서 기억 형성에 미치는 다양한 요소에 대해 알아보았다면, '지금, 여기'에서는 과거로부터 받아들인 정보가 현재의 우리에게 어떠한 영향을 미쳤고, 그 영향으로 형성된 우리의 기억은 어떠한 방식으로 발현되고 있는지 알아보고자 한다.

[4]
앙리 베르그송, 『물질과 기억』, 박종원 옮김(서울: 아카넷, 2005), 256–258.

지금, 여기

기억은 사회나 타인과 같은 자신 주변의 외부적인 요소뿐 아니라 시간에도 영향을 받는다. 과거의 정보가 현재 우리의 기억을 형성하고 있기 때문이다. '역사는 승리자의 기록'이라는 로마 속담과 같이 우리가 현재 알고 있는 과거의 기록은 특정 계층의 매우 한정적인 시각에서 추려진 정보만 전해진 것이다. 그렇기에 현재 우리가 기억하고 있는 것들에 대해 재고해 볼 필요가 있다. 과거가 전해준 정보는 무엇인지, 그리고 그것을 바탕으로 우리는 어떤 기억을 형성했는지에 대해서 말이다.

베르그송에 따르면 시간은 끊임없이 변화하는 상태로서, 한 지점으로 분리되지 않는 지속 안에 과거, 현재, 미래가 공존한다. 한때는 현재였지만 지나가 버린 과거와 미래의 방향성이 함께 공존하고 있는 지속의 상태가 현재이다.[4] 현재의 우리는 과거와 미래 사이의 시간 속에 있는 존재로서 현재 우리가 남기는 정보와 그에 따른 기억의 방향성에 따라 미래의 기억이 달라질 것이다. 이 때문에 우리는 미래 세대에게 정보를 남기기에 앞서 현재 우리가 기억하는 것과 그 방식을 진단해보아야 한다.

과거를 기억하는 방식으로는 회상, 공감, 재고, 반추 등이 있을 것이다. 그중 세실리아 비쿠냐는 공감의 방식으로 자신의 기억을 뒤돌아본다. 칠레 출신의 작가는 인권, 환경, 문화와 같은 동시대 이슈를 퍼포먼스, 설치, 영상, 공예 등의 작업으로 선보이고 있다. 자신의 신념에 따라 목소리를 내는 것에 망설임이 없는 그는 1970년대 초 라틴 아메리카에서 최초로 민주 선거를 통해 당선된 사회주의 정당 출신 대통령 살바도르 아옌데 정권에 반대하며 1973년 아우구스토 피노체트 국방장관이 일으킨 칠레 쿠데타에 저항하다가 결국 추방당한다.

이번 전시에서 소개된 〈나의 베트남 이야기〉(2021)는 자신이 칠레에서 추방되었던 기억을 바탕으로 한다. 작가가 칠레에서 맞서 싸웠던 정치 폭력, 쿠데타로 황폐해진 삶의 터전, 그리고 희생된 수많은 사람 등에 대한 기억을 베트남 전쟁 중 미군에 의해 발생한 미라이 학살을 통해 떠올린다. 영상은 베트남 전쟁의 비극과 희생된 사람들의 이야기, 그리고 그들을 추모하기 위해 제작한 자신의 작품과 전시를 소개하는 내용으로 구성된다.

이 과정에서 우리는 작가가 직접 경험한 기억과 간접 경험으로 획득한 기억이 교차 되면서 발생하는 공감을 볼 수 있다. 그 공감의 매개체가 되는 것은 작가가 베트남 전쟁의 참상을 사진으로 보고 피해자를 추모하기 위해 자신의 손목에 오랫동안 묶고 다녔던 붉은색 스카프이다. 이후 이 붉은색 스카프는 2020년 10월 칠레 산티아고에서

[3]
Kim Ock Kyoung, "Memory and the Self-Identity of Modern Individual in Locke," *Sogang Journal of Philosophy*, vol. 42 (2015), 262–264.

[4]
Henri Bergson, *Matter and Memory*, trans. Park Jongwon (Seoul: Acanet, 2005), 256–258.

in the context of particular societies and relationships. According to John Locke, who formulated the theory of the liberal modern individual, memory is a linchpin of personal identity, where individual identity is identity based on one's own experiences and recollections.[3] Conversely, the memories formed in this way go on to influence our future experiences and memories. From this, we can surmise that identity and memory formation are closely interlinked, and that the various social elements that determine identity are also in a relationship of mutual influence.

While the section "My Your Memory" examines the different elements that affect memory formation, "Here and Now" explores how information from the past influences us today, and how our own memories manifest as they are shaped by those influences.

Here and Now

In addition to external factors that surround us, such as society and other people, memory is also influenced by time—for information from the past comes to shape our memories today. A Roman proverb states that "history is a record of the victors"—and, indeed, the records of the past that we know today reflect only information filtered through the very limited perspective of a particular segment. In that sense, we need to reconsider the things we currently remember, especially in terms of what information has been passed on from the past and what sorts of memories we have created on that basis.

Henri Bergson described time as a constantly transforming state, where past, present, and future coexist in a continuum that cannot be separated into single points; the present is an ongoing state that coexists with the direction of the future and a past that was once the present but has since passed by.[4] We current exist as entities in a time between past and future, while future memories will differ according to the information we leave behind and the resulting direction of memory. For that reason, we need to assess what we remember and how before we begin passing information on to future generations.

Some of the ways in which we remember the past include recollection, sympathy, reconsideration, and rumination. Artist Cecilia Vicuña reflects on her own memories through an approach based on sympathy. Hailing from Chile, the artist has shared work in genres including performance, installation, film, and crafts as she addresses contemporary issues such as human rights, the environment, and culture. As someone who has never hesitated to speak out according to her convictions, Vicuña was ultimately expelled from her homeland for resisting a 1973 coup d'état in Chile by then-Secretary of Defense Augusto Pinochet against the administration of Salvador Allende, who in the early 1970s had become the first socialist president democratically elected in Latin America.

My Vietnam Story (2021), which features in this exhibition, is based on her memory of being expelled from Chile. Through the lens of the My Lai massacre committed by US troops during the Vietnam War, the artist revisits her memories of the political violence she fought against in Chile, the livelihoods left devastated by the coup, and the countless lives that were lost. The film consists of stories about the tragedies of the Vietnam War and the people who were killed, along with an introduction to the artwork and exhibition that Vicuña created to remember them.

In the process, we can witness the sympathy that arises as memories of the artist's

[5]
Paul Ricœur, *La Mémoire,
l'Histoire, l'Oubli*
(Paris: Editions Seuil, 2000)

'라 카사 데 라스 레코히다스'라는 페미니스트 집단이 주도하여 진행된 칠레 반정부시위에서 '우리는 가능한 것의 눈에 보이는 맥박'(Somos el visible pulso de lo posible)이라는 세실리아의 시구가 적힌 거대한 붉은색 천을 행진에 사용하면서 칠레의 저항에 대한 의지와 승리의 상징성을 새로이 획득하게 된다. 이처럼 서로 닮아 있는 듯하지만, 지역, 문화, 시대 등이 다른 두 사건이 기억의 매개체를 공유하면서 지나가 버린 미라이 학살에 대한 작가의 먼 과거의 기억이 현재로 소환된다.

아크람 자타리는 아랍 문화권에 대한 일반적인 편견에 대해 지적하며, 특정 관점으로부터 형성된 편향된 기억을 이야기한다. 작가는 자신이 성장한 아랍 문화에 근간을 두고 사진, 영상 등과 같은 시각 자료를 수집하여 작업의 소재로 삼는다. 그는 주로 레바논 전쟁 이후 문화, 정치, 경제 등 사회 전반 나타나는 현상을 탐구하는데, 특히 대중매체가 갈등과 전쟁을 묘사하는 양상과 현재 중동 분열의 맥락에서 바라본 저항 운동의 논리, 그리고 종교적 근본주의에 관심이 있다.

〈스크립트〉(2018)도 영상을 수집하는 과정을 거쳐 제작한 작품이다. 작가는 유튜브에서 '아들과 아버지'를 검색해서 찾은 영상 중, 중동에서 제작된 많은 수의 영상 속 이슬람교도가 새벽, 낮, 오후, 일몰 직후, 야간 이렇게 하루에 총 다섯 번 수행하는 기도 의식인 '살라트'의 장면을 담고 있는 것을 발견하였다. 그리고 기도 의식을 수행하는 아버지를 장난치며 방해하는 아이들의 모습이 담긴 영상이 많다는 사실 또한 알게되었다. 소재를 찾아내는 이러한 방식은 같은 주제에 대해 기억을 담아내는 매체인 영상을 다량 수집하고, 그 안에서 문화와 기억의 보편성을 찾아내는 것이라고 할 수 있다.

이 작품은 평범한 가정에서 살라트를 수행하는 아버지와 장난치는 두 아들의 풍경을 담고있다. 아랍권에서 성장하지 않은 사람들에게 아랍 문화는 다소 폐쇄적이고, 가부장적일 것이라는 편견이 있는 것이 사실이다. 하지만 이런 오해와는 달리 아랍 문화권의 사람들은 그들의 신념과 문화를 지켜가면서 평범하게 살아가고 있는 사람들일 뿐이다. 그들에게 기도 의식은 일상 속에서 비언어적인 방식으로 전승하는 기억이다. 인간은 기억을 통해 전승된 내용으로 문화적 가치를 이어가고, 이는 과거에 대한 기억 없이는 현재를 인식할 수 없고, 나아가 미래도 판단할 수 없다는 폴 리쾨르의 말처럼 문화의 가치를 이어가는 방식이다.[5] 작가는 이 작품을 통해 우리의 아랍 문화에 대한 편견은 그야말로 우리가 쉽게 노출되는 대중매체에 의해 형성된 것이라고 지적하면서 특히, 서구중심주의와 자본주의의 논리에 따라 전쟁과 갈등으로 묘사하는 것에 영향을 받은 아랍 문화에 대한 우리의 편향적인 기억에 대해 재고해 볼 것을 제안한다.

시프리앙 가이야르는 과거의 정보를 현재의 관점과 가치에 따라 재평가하고 새로운 가치를 부여하는 방식의 기억법을 보여준다. 회화, 조각, 사진, 비디오, 퍼포먼스 등 다양한 매체를 다루어 온 프랑스 출신 작가는 인간이 자연에 남긴 근대 건축 문명의 숭고함과 자신이 어린 시절 즐기던 하위문화를 작품에 교차시킴으로써 동시대 문화에 대한 양면적인 시선을 드러낸다. 작가가 세상을 바라보는 이러한

[5]
Paul Ricœur, *La Mémoire,
l'Histoire, l'Oubli*
(Paris: Editions Seuil, 2000).

own experiences intersect with other memories that she acquired through indirect experience. The medium for that sympathy is a red scarf that the artist long wore around her wrist after seeing photographs documenting the horrors of the Vietnam War. This red scarf that served as her medium for remembrance of Vietnam once again came to symbolize victory and a commitment to resistance in Chile when large red banners bearing Vicuña's words *Somos el visible pulso de lo possible* ("We are the visible pulse of the possible") were used in a march as part of anti-government protests spearheaded by the feminist group La Casa de las Recogidas in Santiago in October 2020. In this way, the artist's memories of the past My Lai massacre are summoned back into the present as the same medium of memory is shared between two seemingly similar yet different incidents.

Akram Zaatari comments on general preconceptions about the Arab cultural world, focusing on the biased memories that are formed from a particular perspective. Basing his work on the Arab culture in which he was raised, Zaatari assembled visual data such as photographs and films to use as material for his work. In particular, he explores the phenomena that have emerged across society in the wake of the war in Lebanon, including the areas of culture, politics, and the economy. He is especially interested in how conflict and war are depicted in mass media, and in religious fundamentalism and the logic of resistance movements as seen in the context of the current divisions in the Middle East.

The Script (2018) was likewise created out of a process of collecting film footage. Among the many videos posted from the Middle East that he found by entering the search term "father and son" on YouTube, the artist sought out ones that showed scenes of *salat*: the ritual prayer that is performed five times daily by Muslims in the early morning, at midway, in the afternoon, just after sunset, and at night. He also found numerous videos showing children playfully disrupting their father's attempts to perform the prayers. This method of tracking down material could be seen as one of assembling numerous videos as media for capturing memories of the same topic, and of seeking out the universality of culture and memory within.

The work shows an ordinary family scene, where the father is performing his salat while his two sons play. Among people who did not grow up in the Arab world, there is a preconception of Arab culture as being rather insular and patriarchal. Contrary to this misconception, however, ordinary Arabs are simply people living ordinary lives while observing their convictions and culture. To them, the prayer ritual is a form of memory passed down non-linguistically within everyday life—reflecting the method of perpetuating cultural values articulated by Paul Ricœur, who said that human beings sustain their cultural values by means of content transmitted through memory, and that they can neither recognize the present nor judge the future without memories of the past.[5] As Zaatari points out how our preconceptions about the Arab world are shaped by the mass media we are so often exposed to, he suggested that we should reconsider the bias in our memories of Arab culture, which have been influenced by depictions of war and conflict in accordance with Western-centric and capitalist attitudes.

Cyprien Gaillard presents a method of remembering in which we reassess past information and assign new value to it based on our present-day perspectives and values. The French artist has worked in a wide range of media including painting, sculpture, photography, film, and performance, as he presents an ambivalent attitude

시선은 작가는 미니멀리즘, 반달리즘, 낭만주의, 대지예술을 관통하는 예술세계를 가졌다는 평가를 받게 한다.

〈호수 아치〉(2007)는 1978부터 1982년까지 스페인 출신의 포스트모더니즘을 대표하는 세계적인 건축가 리카르도 보필이 파리 근교 신도시 계획의 일환으로서 설계한 '호수의 아케이드'를 배경으로 한다. 이 건축물은 완공 직후만 해도 '대중을 위한 베르사유'라고 불릴 정도로 오스만 건축양식과 보필의 독특한 건축세계가 합쳐져 걸작을 만들어 냈다고 칭송을 받았다. 하지만 시간이 지남에 따라 상념적인 도시계획, 상업시설 부재, 건물을 둘러싼 고인 호숫물에 의한 오염, 그리고 단조롭고 간결함을 추구했던 일반 시민들의 미감과 맞지 않는 건물 양식 등으로 외면 받게 되었다.

작가는 건물 앞 호숫가에서 어린 시절부터 즐겼던 다이빙을 하며 시간을 보내려고 했지만, 물의 깊이를 가늠하지 않고 들어간 탓에 얼굴 전체에 피범벅을 하고 물 밖으로 나온다. 그런 그의 배경으로 보이는 건물이 과거가 남긴 정보의 한 유형이라고 한다면, 한때 장엄한 인간의 의지로 남긴 정보가 시대가 변화함에 따라 쓸모 없어진 것을 상징한다고 할 수 있다. 피범벅이 된 작가 또한 한 치 앞도 볼 수 없는 인간의 어리석음을 나타내고, 건축물의 역사와 작가의 퍼포먼스가 절묘하게 결합 되어 현재의 우리는 과거의 위대한 유산(정보)을 현재의 가치로 재평가하고 새로운 가치를 부여하여 기억으로 형성한다는 상기시킨다.

앞선 작가들이 사회나 타인이 남긴 외부의 것에 의한 자신의 기억을 이야기했다면, 루이즈 부르주아는 자신의 내면이 남긴 기억에 집중했다. "우리가 시간을 축적하는 것은 경험을 축적하는 것이라는 시간 속의 경험을 기억하는 것이다."[6] 라는 호르헤 보르헤스의 말처럼 작가의 작업에는 평생의 경험을 통해 형성된 기억과 시간이 흐름에 따라 그 기억이 희석되고, 변화해가는 과정이 여실히 드러난다. 스스로 기억과 공간의 수집가라고 칭했던 부르주아가 평생의 작업 주제로 삼았던 '기억'은 어머니의 모성애에 대한 기억과 경의, 아버지의 외도로 인한 상처와 트라우마, 삶의 모순과 배신 등과 같은 경험으로부터 기인한다. 그는 작품의 물리적 형체를 자신의 신체와 동일시하며 경험에 대한 기억과 그로 인해 느꼈던 감정을 작품에 여실히 투영해왔다. 그의 작품은 페미니즘적인 관점에서 분석되곤 하지만, 부르주아는 자신의 작품들은 단지 여성인 자신의 이야기일 뿐이라고 말하면서 연민, 아픔, 상처, 용서, 화해 등 내면의 감정이 드러나는 자전적인 작품을 지속했다.[7]

판화 연작인 〈코바늘〉(1998)은 직조가 잘 드러나는 붉은색 실선으로 기하학적 패턴을 표현한 작품이다. 대대로 양탄자 수선 사업을 했던 집안에서 태어난 그에게 바느질은 마음을 정화하기 위한 수행과도 같았다. 특히 천과 천을 이어 틈을 메워주는 바느질의 상징적인 반복성은 유년시절 상처 난 그의 마음을 치유해주는 역할을 했다.[8] 작품에 사용한 붉은색은 그가 정상인 것, 피, 고통, 폭력, 위험, 수치심, 질투, 원한, 비난 등의 단어로 치환하여 표현했던 색이었으며, 이 단어들로 표현된 감정들이 일상에 만연하다고 생각했다.[9] 과거, 현재, 미래를 관통하는 시간의 연속성에도 관심이 많았던 그에게 현재의 일상은 과거로부터 온 것이었다. 따라서 붉은색에

[6]
호르헤 루이스 보르헤스, 『영원성의 역사』, 박병규, 박정원, 최이슬기, 이경민 옮김(서울: 민음사, 2018), 61.

[7]
Beatriz Colomina, Louise Bourgeois: Memory and Architecture (Madrid: Museo Nacional Centro de Arte Reina Sofía, 2000), 29–47.

[8]
"내가 어렸을 때, 우리 가족 중 여자들은 모두 바늘을 사용했다. 나는 항상 바늘의 매력과 마술적 힘에 끌려 있었다. 바늘은 손상을 치유하는 데 쓰인다. 그것은 관대하다. 그것은 결코 호전적이지 않다. 그것은 핀이 아니다." Christiane Meyer-Thoss, Louise Bourgeois: Designing For Free Fall (Zurich: Ammann, 1992), 178.

[9]
Louise Bourgeois, Louise Bourgeois: Oeuvres récentes (Bordeaux: CAPC Musée d'art Contemporain de Bordeaux, 1998), 40.

[6]
Jorge Luis Borges, *A History of Eternity*, trans. Park Byongkyu, Park Jeongwon, Choi-Lee Seulgi & Lee Gyeongmin (Seoul: Minumsa, 2018), 61.

[7]
Beatriz Colomina, *Louise Bourgeois: Memory and Architecture* (Madrid: Museo Nacional Centro de Arte Reina Sofía, 2000), 29–47.

[8]
"When I was growing up, all the women in my house were using needles. I've always had a fascination with the needle, the magic power of the needle. The needle is used to repair the damage. It's a claim to forgiveness. It is never aggressive, it's not a pin." Christiane Meyer-Thoss, *Louise Bourgeois: Designing for Free Fall* (Zurich: Ammann, 1992), 178.

on contemporary culture through his juxtaposition of the sublimity of the modern architectural achievements that humankind has left upon nature on one hand, and the subculture that the he himself enjoyed in his youth on the other. This perspective has resulted in Gaillard being described as an artist with an artistic body of work spanning the realms of minimalism, vandalism, romanticism, and land art.

His work *The Lake Arches* (2007) takes place at Les Arcades du Lac, which was designed between 1978 and 1982 as part of a "new town" plan on the outskirts of Paris by Ricardo Bofill, a world-renowned Spanish architect who was a prominent practitioner of postmodernism. At the time of its completion, the structure was praised as a masterwork—a "Versailles for the public" that combined Ottoman architectural style with Bofill's unique architectural vision. But over time, it fell into disfavor due to the conceptual nature of the urban planning, the lack of commercial facilities, pollution of the stagnant lake water surrounding the structure, and the building's style being unsuited to the aesthetic of ordinary people, who favored monotony and concision.

The artist hopes to be able to spend some time diving at the lake next to the structure, enjoying a pastime from his childhood. But he misjudges the depth of the water and emerges with his face covered in blood. If the building visible behind him is seen as a form of information left over from the past, then this could be taken as a symbolic representation of the way that information passed along based on grand human intentions ends up rendered useless by the changes in the times. The bloodied artist represents the foolishness of human beings unable to look ahead for even a moment, while the delicate combination of the structure's history and the artist's performance evokes the way in which people today form memories of the great legacies (information) of the past in a way that assigns them new value and reappraises them according to current values.

While the aforementioned artists relate their own memories based on external things left behind by society or by other people, Louise Bourgeois focuses on memories left behind within herself. Jorge Luis Borges writes, "When we accumulate time, we are remembering the experiences within time as an accumulation of experiences."[6] In Bourgeois's work, we vividly see both memories formed through a life of experience and the process of those memories becoming diluted and transformed over time. The memories here—a lifelong theme in the work of Bourgeois, who referred to herself as a "collector of memories and time"—arise out of her memories of and respect for her mother's love, as well as experiences of the scars and trauma of her father's infidelity and the contradictions and betrayals of life. Equating the physical form of her artwork with her own body, she vividly projected her memories of certain experiences and the emotions that she felt as a result. While her work has often been analyzed from a feminist perspective, she insisted that they merely represented her own story as a woman, while continuing to create autobiographical work that showed inner emotions such as compassion, pain, trauma, forgiveness, and reconciliation.[7]

Bourgeois's print series *Crochet* (1998) is a work that presents geometric patterns produced with red thread, the texture of which is clearly visible. For the artist—whose family had spent generations in the business of repairing carpets—sewing was a form of practice to cleanse her mind. The symbolic repetitiveness of sewing in particular, with the joining of fabric and the filling of the spaces in between, served a healing role amid the scars of her childhood.[8] The red that she uses in the work was transposed into

[10]
김현석, 김효숙, 「비디오 아트에서 시간과 기억 이미지-베르그손의 시간 개념을 중심으로 비디오 작품 사례분석」, 『예술과 미디어』, 15권, 4호(2016), 57-58.

대한 부정적인 감정은 과거의 상처와 트라우마로 인해 형성된 감정을 나타낸다고 볼 수 있으며, 시작과 끝을 알 수 없는 실의 속성과 작품 속 기하학적인 패턴은 시간의 연속성을 상징하는 것이다.

'지금, 여기'에서 우리가 기억하는 과거와 기억방식에 대해 살펴보았다. 이 섹션에서 우리가 지금, 여기에 존재하기에 이미 알고 있는 과거-현재에 걸친 이야기를 주로 다뤘다면, '그때, 그곳'에서는 도래하게 될 미래 세대가 현재 우리가 남기는 정보를 통해 형성하게 될 기억은 어떤 모습일지 현재-미래에 걸친 관점에서 상상해 보고자 한다.

그때, 그곳

현재 우리가 남기는 정보는 미래 세대의 기억 형성에 근간이 될 것이다. 단순히 정보만 영향을 미치는 것이 아니라 기억하는 방식 자체도 정보의 한 유형으로 전달될 것이다. 그렇기에 우리가 과거의 정보를 어떻게 기억해서 미래 세대에게 전달할 것인지에 대해 전달자의 관점에서 고민해보아야 한다.

언어에 의존했던 정보를 전달하는 매체가 최근에는 상당히 다양해졌다. 특히 영상 매체가 굳건하게 예술의 한 장르로 자리매김하면서 작품이 함의하는 서사가 풍부해지기도 했다. 시청각 요소를 담아낼 수 있는 영상 매체는 '정념'을 더 잘 담아낼 수 있다고 여겨지기도 하지만, 기억을 영상으로 시각화한다고 해서 그것을 정확하게 구현해낸다고는 할 수 없을 것이다. 기억은 원래 비정형적이고, 추상적이기 때문이다. 이와 같은 맥락으로 프랑스의 저명한 비디오아트 연구자 프랑스와즈 파르페는 비디오 이미지의 비-고정적인 특징은 현실이 축소된 이미지이기 때문이라고 말하면서, 비디오가 현실을 완벽하게 재현할 수 없기에 발생하는 결핍은 우리의 기억 이미지와 닮았다고 말한다.[10] 파르페가 말한 것처럼 기억 이미지와 유사한 영상 매체를 통해 정보를 남김으로써 우리는 미래 세대에게 단순한 언어에 의한 기록이 아니라 생동하는 정보를 남겨줄 수 있게 되었다.

기억을 담지하는 대표적인 예술 매체인 영상을 이용하여 특정 사건을 재구성한 작가로는 안리 살라와 송주원이 있다. 이들은 자신이 직접 경험하지 않은 과거의 사건을 작품으로 구현해냈다. 사건을 직접 경험하지 않았지만, 남겨진 기록을 학습하고, 기록된 정보 간의 공백을 상상으로 메우는 작품을 선보였다. 이중 안리 살라는 세대, 지역, 문화의 경계를 뛰어넘으며 과거 사건에 접근하기를 시도했다. 그는 지역적, 사상적 노마드를 자처하는 알바니아 출신 작가다. 그가 지역적, 사상적 노마드가 될 수 있었던 배경은 알바니아의 현대사와 결을 함께한다. 문화적으로 알바니아는 과거 로마와 오스만제국의 지배를 번갈아 받아 기독교와 이슬람 문화가 융합된 독자적인 문화를 발전시켰다. 사회·정치적으로는 제2차 세계대전의 종전과 함께 이탈리아로부터 독립한 후 국제 외교사회와 오랫동안 교류를 단절한 채 정통 사회주의 체제를 고수하며 유럽에서 가장 폐쇄적이고, 가난한 나라였다. 1990년대에는 오랫동안 알바니아를 장악했던 독재정권과 엄격한 사회주의가

[9]
Louise Bourgeois, *Louise Bourgeois: Oeuvres récentes* (Bordeaux: CAPC Musée d'art Contemporain de Bordeaux, 1998), 40.

[10]
Kim Hyunsuk, Kim Hyosook, "Time and Memory Image in Video Art–Analysis of Video Art Cases Focusing on Bergson's Time Concept," *Art & Media*, vol. 15, no. 4 (2016), 57–58.

words such as "normal," "blood," "pain," "violence," "danger," "shame," "jealousy," "resentment," and "criticism"; the artist saw the feelings expressed through these words as being pervasive in our lives.[9] As someone interested in the continuity of time through past, present, and future, she saw the daily experience of today as something with origins in the past. In that sense, the negative feelings associated with the color red can be seen as representing emotions formed through past scars and trauma, while the indeterminate endings and beginnings of the patterns and the qualities of the thread come to symbolize the continuity of time.

The section "Here and Now" examines the forms of the past that we remember and our ways of remembering. While this section focuses mainly on stories spanning the past and present, which we already know of because we exist here and now, the section "That Time, That Place" adopts a perspective spanning the present and future as it attempts to imagine what sorts of memories will be formed by future generations through the information that we today leave behind.

That Time, That Place

The information that we leave behind today will become a basis for future generations to form their own memories. It is not merely information that will have an influence—our ways of remembering will also be passed on as a form of information. In that sense, we must think from the perspective of "transmitters" about how we will remember past information and pass it on to future generations.

Where media for relaying information once relied on language, their approaches have recently become quite diverse. In particular, the establishment of the video medium as a full-fledged genre of art has resulted in an enriching of the narratives contained with artistic work. With its ability to capture both audio and visual elements, the film medium is seen as capable of better capturing "sentiments"—but visualizing memories in film does not necessarily mean that we are representing those memories accurately. Memory is inherently amorphous and abstract. Along these lines, the eminent French video art scholar Françoise Parfait attributed the non-fixed nature of the video image to its being a reduced image of the reality, arguing the deficiencies that arise from video's inability to perfectly represent reality are similar to our remembered images.[10] As Parfait suggests, when we leave information behind through a cinematic medium that is similar to the remembered image, what we are able to pass on to future generations is not a mere record in words, but information that is vividly alive.

Anri Sala and Song Joowon are two artists who reconstruct particular incidents through the use of film as a representative artistic medium for containing memory. In their work, they recreate past incidents that they did not experience themselves. Despite not having personally experienced the events, they pore over the surviving records, while using their imagination to fill in the gaps in the recorded information. Sala has attempted an approach to past incidents that transcends boundaries of generations, regions, and cultures. The Albanian artist describes himself as a regional and philosophical nomad. Indeed, his ability to become a regional and philosophical nomad has been influenced by Albania's modern history and character. Culturally, Albania has developed a unique culture blending aspects of Christian and Islamic culture due to its alternate rule by the Roman and Ottoman Empires. Sociopolitically, it has been the most insular and impoverished country in Europe: after achieving independence from Italy at

몰락하고, 새로 도입된 자본주의 시장경제 시스템에 국민이 혼란을 겪었다. 1997년에는 거의 전 국민을 상대로 한 알바니아 금융사기 사건까지 발생하면서 국가 경제사회가 휘청거리기도 했다. 이런 혼란의 알바니아를 뒤로하고 작가는 22세의 나이에 프랑스로 유학을 떠났다. 엄격한 사회주의부터 자유로운 민주주의까지 정체성이 형성되는 시기에 모두 경험한 작가는 자연스레 지역적, 사상적 경계를 자유로이 넘나들며 인류의 보편적인 감정을 작품으로 이야기하기 시작했다. 이러한 작가의 개인적 배경과 작업 방향은 직접 경험하지 못했고, 문화적 배경도 다른 사라예보 포위전을 배경으로 한 영상 작품 〈붉은색 없는 1395일〉(2011)을 제작할 수 있게 해주었을 것이다.

사라예보 포위전은 보스니아 내전(1992–1995) 중 발생한 현대사에서 가장 긴 포위전 중 하나이며, 약 20만 명의 희생자, 약 230만 명의 난민을 발생 시켜 나치 학살 이후 유럽에서 최초로 발생한 대량학살로 기록된다. 사건의 발단은 보스니아가 유고슬라비아로부터 독립하는 과정에서 발생한 사르비아계 민족과 다른 민족들 간의 갈등이었다. 당시 세르비아계 출신이었던 유고슬라비아 대통령은 세르비아 민족부흥을 주창하며 정책을 펼쳤기 때문에 보스니아 내 세르비아계 민족은 독립을 반대했다. 반면 다른 민족은 독립을 찬성하면서 생긴 민족갈등이 무력전으로 이어진 것이다. 유고슬라비아의 전폭적인 지원을 받는 세르비아 민병대는 각종 무기를 동원하여 보스니아 정부군을 공격했고, 결국 사라예보를 포위한다. 그들은 시가전, 폭격뿐 아니라 고층 건물에 스나이퍼를 배치하여 거리의 민간인을 무차별하게 저격했다. 그 때문에 당시 거리에는 '스나이퍼 조심'(Pazi Snajper)라는 문구를 흔히 볼 수 있었고, 그 속에서 시민들은 일상을 이어가야만 했다. 당시 그들이 선택한 생존법은 길목을 건널 때마다 건물 그림자에 숨어서 동태를 살피다가 황급히 뛰어서 건너가는 것이었다.

〈붉은색 없는 1395일〉은 도심을 가로지르는 여자 주인공의 여정을 따라가며 위험한 건널목을 지날 때마다 내비치는 긴장된 눈빛과 몸짓, 전력 질주로 인한 가쁜 호흡 등을 보여주고, 이 긴장된 호흡에 맞추어 작곡된 곡을 연주하는 관현악단의 모습을 교차 편집한다. 영상 중반에 여자 주인공은 맞은편에서 달려온 남성과 눈이 마주친다. 그리고 서로 말없이 숨을 고르며 잠시 머물다가 또다시 전력 질주를 시작한다. 이는 설명하지 않아도 한 사회에서 통용되는 것들이 쌓여 자연스럽게 형성되는 집단 기억을 표현한다. 작가는 역사적인 사건을 작품의 소재로 많이 사용하는데, 특히 장소가 함의하는 역사적인 맥락과 음악적 요소는 기억을 소환하는 특유의 방식이라고 할 수 있다. 이는 언어적인 정보만으로는 채워지지 않는 사건에 대한 기억을 오감으로 받아들인 공감각적 정보로 메우려는 작가 고유의 방식이고, 언어가 갖은 힘에 대한 불신의 표현이다.

안리 살라가 지구 반대편의 이야기를 영상 작품으로 제작했다면 송주원은 한국의 과거 사건을 몸의 언어로 재해석하고, 이를 '댄스필름'(dance films)으로 제작했다. 안무가이자 영화감독인 그는 공연예술의 전통적 수행 공간인 극장을 벗어나 실내외

the end of World War II, it remained long isolated from interactions with international diplomatic society, adhering instead to an authentically socialist regime. During the 1990s, the dictatorship that had ruled Albania for so long collapsed, along with its strict brand of socialism; the newly adopted capitalist market economy system left the people experiencing chaos. Albania's economy and society were dealt a further blow in 1997 with a financial pyramid scheme crisis that affected almost the entire population. Leaving behind a country in tumult, the artist went to study in France at the age of 22. After he had experienced everything from strict socialism to free democracy during the time his identity was taking shape, it was a natural progression for the artist to freely alternate across regional and philosophical borders as he created work that expressed universal human emotions. This direction in the artist's work may have been what allowed him to create *1395 Days Without Red* (2011), a film set against the backdrop of the Siege of Sarajevo—an event that the artist had not experienced himself, and that had taken place in a different cultural milieu.

The Siege of Sarajevo, which occurred amid the Bosnian civil war from 1992 to 1995, was one of the longest sieges in contemporary history. Resulted in around 200,000 deaths and roughly 2.3 million refugees, it is remembered as the first large-scale massacre in Europe since the Nazi Holocaust. The situation originated in conflicts between Serbians and other ethnic groups when Bosnia was gaining independence from Yugoslavia. Serbians in Bosnia were opposed to independence due to the policies of the Serbian President of Yugoslavia, who was proclaiming a Serbian "national revival." Other ethnic groups supported independence, and the resulting national frictions eventually erupted into warfare. Operating with Yugoslavia's full-scale support, Serbian militia members used various weapons to attack Bosnian government forces, and they ultimately placed the capital city of Sarajevo under siege. In addition to street fighting and bombing attacks, they also placed snipers in tall buildings to fire indiscriminately on civilians in the streets. This resulted in messages of "beware of snipers" (*Pazi snajper*) becoming a common sight in the streets—while ordinary people had to go about their lives amid all of this. One survival strategy that they adopted at the time was to conceal themselves in the shadows of buildings whenever they crossed the street, checking for activities before racing to the other side.

1395 Days Without Red follows the journey of one woman, showing the tense gazes and gestures at every perilous crosswalk, along with her gasping breaths as she races with all her strength. This is intercut and juxtaposed with images of an orchestra playing a composition designed to correspond to those anxious breaths. Midway through the film, the woman makes eye contact with a man who has come running from the other side of the street. Without speaking, they wait and catch their breath before beginning another headlong race. This is an expression of the collective memories that naturally form within societies through repeated practices that do not require explanation. Sala often draws upon events from history as material for his work; in particular, the historical contexts associated with places and the musical elements can be seen as his characteristic approach for evoking memory. It is his unique method of using synesthetic information from the five senses to fill in the gaps in memories of incidents that are not complete through linguistic information alone—and it is also an expression of his distrust in the power of language.

While Anri Sala created a cinematic work based on a story from the other side of

다양한 장소를 배경으로 한 안무를 영상으로 촬영한 댄스필름을 꾸준히 제작해오고 있다. 2013년 '풍정.각(風情.刻) 프로젝트'를 결성하여 안무가로서 활동을 이어오다가 최근에는 시각예술 영역에서까지 작품이 활발히 소개되면서 시각과 공연예술의 경계를 넘나들고 있다.

작가는 무대가 되는 장소의 시간과 역사를 연구하고 그 맥락에 맞추어 안무를 구성하는 장소 특정적 작품을 주로 선보이고 있는데, ‹뽀루지.물집.사마귀.점›(2021)도 이 같은 성격을 띠는 댄스필름이다. 이 작품의 배경이 되는 곳은 국군광주병원 옛터로, 이곳은 5·18 광주민중항쟁[11] 당시 수많은 시민 부상자들을 치료하던 곳이었다. 현재 병원은 함평으로 옮겨지고, 국군광주병원 옛터는 최근 시민들에게 개방되기 전까지 방치된 채, 40여 년이 지난 지금까지도 진상이 명확하게 규명되지 않은 아픈 역사와 기억을 고스란히 간직하고 있었다.

이곳을 무대로 정한 작가는 당시의 사건과 이 장소의 기억을 연구했지만, 사실적 기록을 연결 짓는 것만으로는 닿을 수 없는 부분에 갈증을 느꼈다. 이 사건을 직접 경험하지 못한 작가는 이 갈증을 상상으로 메우기 시작했고, 그가 해석한 당시의 긴박함, 슬픔, 절망, 우울 등이 안무에 나타난다. 무용수가 보여주는 안무를 따라 병원의 내부를 보게 되는데, 무용수들의 몸짓과 무대로 변모한 공간이 융합되면서 보여주는 필름은 단순히 역사 유적으로만 공간을 바라보는 것이 아니라 우리에게 공간을 세밀히 관찰하고, 그곳에 내포된 이야기를 상상해 보도록 유도한다.

앞선 두 영상이 기억의 시청각 요소를 구체적으로 재현하면서 정보 간 공백을 메워 상상력을 자극했다면, 뮌은 오디토리움 형식을 빌려 기억의 근원적인 불안정성을 표현한다. 김민선, 최문선으로 구성된 듀오 그룹 작가 뮌은 미디어와 사회에 관심을 두고 있으며, 특히 사회에서 드러나는 군중의 행태와 속성, 공공과 공동체, 미디어의 영향으로 형성된 선입견 등에 대해 질문하며 사진, 영상, 인터렉티브 설치 등의 작업을 주로 선보이고 있다. ‹오디토리움(Template A–Z)›(2022)은 기억의 불안정하고 유동적인 속성에 주목하며, 16세기에 고안된 '기억극장'(Theatro della Memoria)의 형식을 빌려 과거의 기억을 현재의 관점으로 재구성한 이미지 결과물을 제시한다. 기억극장은 16세기 초 카밀로라는 사람이 르네상스 시대에 베네치아 궁정에 세운 목조 극장으로 고대로부터 전수된 '기억술'(ars meroriae)을 극장의 형태로 가시화하여 인간의 체험을 분류, 저장, 유통한다. 기억극장에 들어서면 관람자는 무대에 서서 그간 인류가 축적해온 우주의 비밀에 대한 방대한 지식이 체계적으로 분류 기록된 언어와 이미지 자료가 진열되어 있는 관객석을 마주한다.

이러한 기억극장의 형식에 따라 ‹오디토리움(Template A–Z)›도 5개의 '관객석'에 기억의 이미지를 형상화한다. 작가는 머릿속 기억의 공간을 '경이로운 방'이라는 뜻인 '분더캄머'(Wunderkammer)[12] 라고 표현하는데, 2014년 같은 형식의 오디토리움 작품을 제작한 이후 부분적으로 소실되고 추가된 자신들의 분더캄머를 새로운 버전의 작품을 제작함으로써 다시 들춰낸다. 새로운 작품에서는 통계, 플랫폼, 반복소비, 유랑극단, 궤적 등과 같은 주제를 중심으로 45개의 기억의 장면을 연출한다. 이 45개의

[11]
1979년 10월 박정희 대통령이 사망하면서 많은 이들은 군부독재 시대가 막을 내릴 것으로 예상했으나 전두환과 노태우가 주축인 하나회가 군부를 장악하고, 정치적 실세로 등극하는 12·12 사태가 일어나면서 전 국민이 반발하기 시작했다. 당시 광주에서도 전남대학교, 조선대학교 등의 대학생들을 중심으로 시민들이 신군부 규탄 및 민주화 시위를 벌였는데, 신군부는 이를 무력으로 제압하고자 계엄령을 선포하고 공수부대를 투입하여 1980년 5월 19일 시민을 향해 최초로 실탄을 발포한 후부터 21일까지 수많은 시민 사상자를 냈다.

[12]
근대 초기 유럽의 지배층과 학자들이 자신의 저택에 온갖 진귀한 사물들을 수집하여 진열했던 실내공간.

The assassination of South Korean President Park Chunghee in October 1979 was expected to usher an end to the era of military dictatorship. Instead, it led to the Hanahoe ("Group of One"), led by Chun Doo-hwan and Roh Tae-woo, assuming control of the military and political authorities. The situation led to a growing outcry from the public. In Gwangju, members of the public—and students at Chonnam National University and Chosun University in particular—held demonstrations to condemn the military administration and call for democratization. The military government declared martial law and deployed airborne troops to quash the protests. The first use of live ammunition against civilians occurred on May 19, 1980; by May 21, countless citizens had been injured or killed.

the planet, Song Joowon reinterprets incidents from Korea's past through the language of the body, transforming them into "dance films." A choreographer and film director, she has regularly produced dance films that leave behind the traditional performing space of the theater to film choreography against the backdrop of different locations. After establishing the Pung Jeong.Gak Project in 2013 as a base for her choreography activities, she has recently been blurring the boundaries of the visual and performing art through her prolific activities in the visual arts field.

The artist has chiefly presented site-specific work, in which she researches the history and time associated with her setting and develops choreography to suit that context. *Pimple.Blister.Wart.Mole* (2021) is another example of a dance film along these lines. The backdrop for this work is the site of the Former Armed Forces' Gwangju Hospital in Gwangju, a place where many wounded citizens were treated at the time of the Gwangju Uprising of May 1980.[11] The hospital has since been relocated to Hampyeong; prior to its recent reopening to the public, the former site lay in neglect, harboring painful memories and a history that still has not been fully brought to light more than four decades later.

After settling on this site as her backdrop, the artist researched memories of the incident and location. Yet she also yearned to capture aspects that could not be achieved simply by piecing together the fact-based accounts. Not having experienced the incident herself, the artist began filling in the gaps with her own imagination, her choreography incorporating the senses of urgency, sorrow, despair, and melancholy that she read into the events. The viewer sees the hospital's interior through the choreographed movements of a dancer; as the choreography blends with the space that has now transformed into a "stage," the film encourages us to closely observe the setting and imagine the stories contained within it, rather than simply viewing it as the site of a historical episode.

While that video work stimulates the imagination as it concretely represents the auditory and visual elements of memory to fill in information gaps, Mioon uses the auditorium format to show the inherent instability of memory. A duo consisting of artists Minsun Kim and Moonsun Choi, Mioon focuses its attention on media and society, working primarily in genres such as photography, film, and interactive installations as it poses questions about the actions and characteristics of crowds in society; the public realm and communities; and the prejudices that form as a result of media influences. *Auditorium (Template A–Z)* (2002) concentrates on the fluid, unstable aspects of memory, drawing on the format of the Teatro della Memoria (developed during the 16th century) to present images that reconstruct past memories from a present-day vantage point. Dating back to the Renaissance, the Teatro della Memoria was a wooden theater built in the early 16th century in the Venetian palace by Giulio Camillo; it used the theater format to visualize the *ars memoriae* (art of memory) that had been passed down since ancient times, through the classification, storage, and circulation of human experiences. Entering the Teatro della Memoria, the visitor ascended the stage and looked out on the seats, where linguistic and image-based materials were on display, systematically classifying and recording vast volumes of information about the secrets of the universe that had been acquired by human beings over time.

Adopting the same kind of "theater of memory" format, *Auditorium (Template A–Z)* visualizes the images of memory in its five "seats." The artists use the term

장면은 작가의 개인적인 경험과 취향을 바탕으로 한 비정형적인 기억의 찰나를 포착한 것으로, 기억의 표상인 견본들을 조합하여 그림자 극장을 선보인다. 작품의 정면에서 바라본 불투명한 아크릴에 비친 견본들과 빛의 변주는 기억의 서사를 유추할 수 있는 듯 보이지만, 작품 뒤쪽으로 돌아 들어가면 보이는 견본들과 빛이 뒤엉켜 있는 모습은 서사의 내용을 가늠할 수 없게 한다. 또, 빛이 벽면으로 퍼지면서 웅장하게 드러나는 견본들의 그림자까지 합쳐지면서 기억의 모호함, 망각, 왜곡 등을 상징한다. 작가의 기억극장은 견본들을 통해 기억의 유형을 체계화하고, 작품을 마주한 관람객들이 기호화된 장면을 해석하고 재구성할 수 있는 무대를 제시한다.

박혜수는 특유의 작업 방식인 대화를 기반으로 영상과 회화가 지닌 매체의 속성을 이용하여 기억에 접근한다. 작가는 사회가 집단적으로 내포하고 있는 무의식과 개인의 기억과 삶에 대해 질문을 던지고, 응답 내용을 데이터화하여 작가의 조형언어로 해석하는 '대화' 프로젝트를 10여 년간 진행해왔다. 대화는 작가에게 수많은 데이터를 제공하면서 인간의 감정과 사회 공동체가 지니는 보편적인 가치를 탐구할 수 있게 해주는 수단이다. 최근에는 프로젝트의 두 번째 세부 프로젝트인 '굿바이 투 러브'를 통해 사랑이라는 감정을 바탕으로 현대인들의 내밀한 감정과 외로움에 대해 질문하고 있다.

〈기쁜 우리 젊은 날〉(2022)은 첫사랑에 대한 이야기다. 작가는 누구나 하나쯤 간직하고 있는 아련한 첫사랑에 대한 기억을 구로공단 지역을 비롯한 공업 단지의 노동자들에게 묻는다. 1970-1980년대 한국의 주요 산업이었던 제조업의 주역이었던 그들은 젊은 시절 자신이 공장에서 일하게 된 배경부터 이야기하며 옛 날들을 회상하기 시작한다. 이어진 첫사랑에 대한 질문에 쑥스러워하면서도 미소 띤 얼굴로 첫사랑의 외모, 첫 만남, 가슴 떨렸던 사랑 이야기, 그리고 헤어짐과 상처 등을 고백하듯 이야기한다. 그리고 그들의 이야기를 듣고 회화로 첫사랑을 표현하는 함미나 작가의 모습과 첫사랑과의 추억이 서려 있는 장소의 풍경이 무심히 스쳐 지나간다.

젊은 시절 사랑했던 기억은 개인의 역사가 되어 남는다. 이 역사는 자신이 정한 모습과 감정의 테두리에 갇혀 첫사랑의 대상조차도 침범할 수 없는 지극히 주관적인 기억이다. 누구도 사실 여부를 알 수 없는 자신만의 첫사랑에 대한 추억을 묘사하는 방식은 아주 편향적이다. 이는 쟁취의 역사일 수도 있고, 한때 잘나갔던 청년기에 대한 자랑일 수도 있다. 말하자면 자신의 존재를 확인시켜주는 역사인 것이다. 이 때문일까. 이 기억이 후회, 교훈, 자랑스러움, 상처 등의 감정으로 남는다 하더라도 많은 노동자가 첫사랑을 다시 만나는 것에 대해 명확히 답하지 못한다. 자신의 소중한 첫사랑에 대한 기억을 침범당하고 싶지 않아서다.

박혜수는 이 지점에서 그들의 첫사랑의 역사를 회화로 재해석하며 침범해가기 시작한다. 함미나 작가와 협업한 회화 작품 속 이미지는 노동자들이 묘사한 밝고 푸릇했던 첫사랑의 이미지와는 사뭇 다르다. 인터뷰 속 노동자들과 30여 년 정도 차이 나는 후세대의 작가가 그려내는 그들의 사랑 이야기는 어딘가 모르게 침울하게 느껴진다. 이는 미화된 첫사랑의 추억에 가려져 당시의 고단했던 일상과 현실이

[12]
These indoor spaces were kept
by scholars and members of
the ruling class in early modern
Europe to display assembled
rare objects in their homes.

Wunderkammer, or "room of wonders,"[12] to refer to this space of memories within the mind. A previous *Auditorium* work along similar lines was produced in 2014; here, the artists have presented their *Wunderkammer* once again in a newly produced version that has lost some elements and gained others. The new work presents 45 scenes from memory, focusing on topics such as "statistics," "platforms," "repeated consumption," "traveling players," and "trajectories." The 45 scenes capture amorphous moments of remembering based on the artists' personal experiences and tastes, resulting in a shadow theater that brings together "specimens" as representations of memory. The variations in light and the specimens seen through the opaque acrylic from the front of the artwork suggest that it might be possible to infer a narrative of memory—but those who walk behind the work see the specimens and light entangled in such a way that no narrative content can be discerned. Added onto this are the shadows of the specimens that loom majestically as the light radiates to the walls; these symbolize memory's ambiguities, forgetting, and distortion. The artists' theater of memory systematizes the forms of memory through its specimens, providing a stage for viewers of the work to interpret and reconstruct the symbol-ized scenes.

Based on her unique dialogue-centered artistic methods, Park Hyesoo makes use of the properties of the film and painting media to approach the topic of memory. For over a decade, she has been involved in a "dialogue" project that consists of asking questions about individual memories and lives and the unconscious harbored collectively by society, after which she converts the responses into data that she interprets through her own aesthetic language. Dialogue has been a means of providing the artist with large amounts of data, while also allowing her to explore human feelings and the universal values of communities. Recently, she has been using the project's second sub-project, titled "Goodbye to Love," to use the emotion of "love" as a way of interrogating the secret emotions and loneliness of contemporary people.

Our Joyful Young Days (2022) focuses on stories of first love. Park Hyesoo poses questions to workers in industrial districts (including Seoul's Guro Industrial Complex) about their memories of first love—something all of us can dimly recall. The workers—key figures in the manufacturing industries that were Korea's mainstays during the 1970s and 1980s—begin recalling their younger days as they talk about how they ended up working at their factory. Next, they are asked about their experiences of first love, responding with both bashfulness and smiles as they talk about their first love's appearance, how they met, how it felt to be in love, and the painful experience of parting. Intercut with this are images of the artist Ham Mina—who paints the objects of the stories after hearing them—and of the landscapes bearing these memories of first love.

Our memories of young love become our personal history. These histories are an exceedingly subjective realm of memory, framed in the images and emotions that we decide in such a way that even the object of our first love cannot intrude upon them. All of us are very biased in the way that we represent our own memories of first love, being unable to know what is true and what is false. It may be a history of battling, and it may be a way of boasting of the successes of our younger selves. In a word, it is a history that confirms our own existence. Perhaps that explains why many of the workers do not offer a clear answer about whether they wish to reunite with their first love, even when those memories are charged with feelings such as regret, learning, pride, and pain: they do not

함미나 작가의 시선에는 보였기 때문이 아닐까. 카를 만하임에 의하면, 세대는 일정한 나이 격차로 구분된다기보다 집단이 공유하는 경험으로 결정된다. 즉 특정한 사회적, 역사적 위치에서 서로 공유하는 사건, 문화, 그리고 일상적인 경험에 의하여 세대라는 사회적 집단의 정체성이 발달한다.[13] 이런 관점에서 볼 때 함미나 작가는 공단 노동자들과 같은 집단기억을 형성하지 않으며, 그에 따라 정체성도 달리 형성되었을 것이다. 하지만 그러한 점이 작용하여 노동자들은 이제 잊고 지내는 당시의 고단함을 들춰내어 그림에 소환할 수 있었다고 볼 수 있다.

[13]
김계환, 「기억으로서의 영상매체와 기억산업의 문화콘텐츠」, 『한국콘텐츠학회논문지』, 9권, 2호(2009), 167.

그리고 영상 마지막에는 「상록수」가 흘러나온다. 1977년 가수 김민기가 인천의 한 공장에서 근무하며 아침마다 공부를 가르치던 노동자들의 합동결혼식에서 축가로 사용하기 위해 만들었다는 이 노래는 끝내 이루지 못한 사랑 이야기에 쓸쓸함을 더한다.

홍순명은 전통적인 회화 매체를 이용하여 추상적인 찰나의 이미지에 작품을 보는 누군가의 수많은 잠재적 기억을 담아내기를 시도한다. 그는 '부분과 전체'라는 철학적 명제를 회화, 조각, 설치 등의 방식으로 실현한다. 눈에 잘 띄지 않는 주변의 것들에 주목하며 의도적으로 그것의 부분을 크게 확대하는 일명 '사이드 스케이프'(side scape) 작업을 지속해왔다. 작가는 정치, 경제, 사회, 문화 등 다양한 영역의 주제를 사유하고 이를 바탕으로 예술세계를 형성해왔으며, 최근에는 난민 문제에 관심을 두고 작업하고 있다.

바다 풍경을 크게 확대한 회화 작품 〈비스듬한 기억-역설과 연대〉(2022)에는 다양한 기억이 중첩되어 있다. 기억의 발단은 작가가 어린 시절 바닷가에서 익사할 뻔했던 사건이다. 당시 바닷물에 빠져 죽음의 공포를 느꼈던 순간, 수면의 안팎을 넘나들며 보았던 아름다운 풍경이 작가에게 선명한 기억으로 남아있다. 이 기억을 시작으로 바다를 각기 다른 관점에서 바라보는 타인의 기억을 상상하기 시작한다. 프랑스 유학 시절 만났던 베트남 난민 이웃이 탈출하기 위해 필리핀까지 헤엄쳤다는 이야기, 시리아 젊은 남성 난민들이 가족은 배에 태우고 자신은 배의 끝자락을 잡고 헤엄치던 모습이 담긴 뉴스 영상, 난민이 몰려들기 전까지 관광이 주요 지역 산업이었던 그리스의 스킬라 시카미니아스의 그물을 손질하는 늙은 어부의 사진. 작가는 바다에 대한 이들의 기억이 과연 자신이 죽음의 목전에서 보았던 아름다운 풍경과 같았을까라고 자문한다.

끊임없이 생성과 소멸을 반복하며 물결치는 바다를 유동성 없는 미술 매체인 회화 작품에 담은 것은 흘러가는 시간 속의 한순간을 그림에 가둬둔 것과 같다. 이로써 작품 속 멈춰진 바다 이미지는 바다의 속성에서부터 분리되어 하나의 표상으로서 존재하게 된다. 작가는 이 표상에 개인적인 기억에서부터 자신의 기억 속에 있는 타인의 기억, 나아가 작품을 감상하게 될 잠재적 관람객들의 기억까지 겹쳐져 작품이 함의하는 기억의 층위를 더욱 단단히 하고, 각자가 고유의 방식으로 그림 속 표상에 자신의 경험을 투영하여 기억을 소환할 수 있기를 기대한다.

전시는 기억이란 무엇인지, 우리가 기억하고 있는 것은 무엇인지, 또 기억한 것을

[13]
Kim Gyehwan, "Cultural
Contents of Image Texts
and Memory Industry as the
Memory," *The Journal of the
Korea Contents Association*,
vol. 9, no. 2 (2009), 167.

want anyone intruding on their precious memories of first love.

At this point, the artist begins to trespass on their histories of first love by having them reinterpreted through painting. The images in the paintings—collaborations with artist Ham Mina—are quite different from the bright and fresh images of first love that the workers describe. As rendered by an artist from a later generation who is some three decades younger than the workers taking part in the interviews, their love stories seem somehow depressing. Perhaps this is because Ham's gaze captures the difficult lives and conditions at the time, obscured as they are behind the whitewashed memories of first love. Karl Mannheim saw generations as being distinguished less in terms of differences in age than in the experiences collectively shared by their members; in other words, the identities of generations as societal collectives develop through the events, culture, and everyday experiences shared by people in a particular social and historical position.[13] From this perspective, Ham Mina is not someone who forms the same collective memories as the complex workers, and her identity has been differently shaped as a result. At the same time, this very factor appears to be at play as she is able to revisit the struggles that the workers have since forgotten and evoke them in her paintings.

At the end of the film, the song "Sangnoksu (Evergreen)," plays. The song, which is said to have been written by the singer Kim Minki in 1977 for use at a joint wedding ceremony for workers he had been teaching every morning while working at a factory in Incheon—adds an additional plaintive quality to the stories of love unrealized.

Hong Soun attempts to use the traditional medium of painting to present images of abstract moments that capture the various potential memories of all the people who will come to view his work. He applies approaches such as painting, sculpture, and installation to embody the philosophical proposition of "the part and the whole." Focusing on periphery, not-easily-noticed aspects, he has consistently created "side scape" artworks that deliberately magnify those elements. In the past, Hong has contemplated themes in different areas such as politics, the economy, society, and culture, which he has used as a basis for his artistic work; recently, he has been turning his attention to the issue of refugees.

His work *Oblique Memory–Irony and Solidarity* (2022) is a painting that offers a greatly magnified view of a seascape, containing various layers of memory within it. The incident that triggered his memory was his experience of nearly drowning in the sea as a child. At the moment when he was experiencing mortal fear underneath the waves, the beautiful sight that he witnessed flailing up and down over the surface stayed with him as a vivid memory. Using that memory as his basis, he began imagining the memories of different people viewing the surface of the sea and the water underneath from different perspectives: the story of the Vietnamese refugee neighbor the artist met during his studies in France, who swam to the Philippines just to survive; news footage showing young male Syrian refugees allowing their family members to travel on boats while they grabbed the edges and paddled along; the photograph of an old fisher mending nets in Skala Sikaminias, a Greek village where tourism had been the major local industry before refugees began pouring in. The artist asks himself whether their memories of the sea were really the same as the beautiful landscape he saw as he faced his own imminent death.

When the rippling sea, with its constant cycling of creation and destruction, is captured within the non-fluid artistic medium of painting, it is similar to capturing a

어떻게 미래 세대에게 전달해줄 것인지에 대해 질문한다. 이러한 질문을 하는 것은 너무 빨리 변화하는 시대에 잠시 멈춰 서서 우리의 지난 삶의 모습을 되돌아보고, 앞으로 나아가야 할 방향을 모색하기 위함이다. 시대가 부추기는 속도에 자신을 맞추는 것이 당연시되는 요즘, 이 전시가 기억이 남긴 다양한 삶의 모습을 들여다보고, 나아가 자신의 삶도 반추하는 기회가 되어 스스로의 방향성을 찾아가는 첫걸음이 되기를 바란다.

moment from the flow of time and pinning it within the frame. As a result, the suspended image of the sea within the work becomes separated from the sea's nature, existing instead as a representation. Hong Soun's hope is that as this representation overlaps with his own personal memories, the memories of others within his memory, and the memories of the potential viewers who will see his work someday, this will further cement the layers of memory encompassed by his work, so that each individual can project experiences on the representation and summon forth memories in their own unique way.

This exhibition poses questions about what memory is, what it is that we remember, and how the things we remember will be passed down to later generations. The reason it asks these questions is to encourage us to pause and reflect on our own lives to date amid an era where everything is changing so quickly, while considering what direction we will need to travel in the future. At a time when it is taken for granted that we will match our own tempo that the era's demands, this exhibition can hopefully be an opportunity to look back at the different images of life that memory has left behind—and to ponder our own lives as we take the first step in finding our own direction.

묻혀있는 기억을 발굴하기: 미술과 기억

Uncovering Buried Memories: Art and Recollection

김남시
이화여자대학교 예술학 전공 교수

Kim Namsee
Professor of Studies in Visual Arts,
Ewha Womans University

서울대학교 미학과 졸업,
베를린 훔볼트 대학 문학학과
박사. 2015년부터 이화여대
조형예술대학 교수로 재직하고
있다. 「과거를 어떻게 (대)할
것인가. 발터 벤야민의 회억
개념」을 비롯해 다수의 발터
벤야민 연구 논문을 발표했고,
프리드리히 키틀러 『축음기,
영화, 타자기』, 아비 바르부르크
『뱀 의식』, 마르쿠스 가브리엘
『예술의 힘』 등을 번역하였다.

Kim Namsee graduated from the
department of aesthetics of Seoul
National University and earned
a doctoral degree in literature
from Humboldt University
of Berlin. Since 2015, he has
been a professor at the Ewha
Womans University College of
Art and Design. He has published
numerous papers on the work
of Walter Benjamin, including
"How to Handle the Past: The
Concept of 'Eingedenken' by
Walter Benjamin." He also
translated *Gramophone, Film,
Typewriter* by Friedrich Kittler,
The Serpent Ritual by Aby
Warburg, and *The Power of Art*
by Markus Gabriel.

기억은, 현재에 몰두하지 않아도 되는 하릴없는 사람들이 지나가버린 과거의
일을 그리워하거나 자기연민으로 가득한 회환에 잠길 때, 아니면 왕년의 영광을
떠벌리며 거들먹거릴 때나 필요한 누추하고 비루하며 쓸모없는 것일까? 기억에
잠기는 건 과거에 매달리느라 더 중요하고 시급한 현재에 등을 돌리는, 한가롭고
비생산적인 소일거리일까? 이런 질문은 지나간 것들에 대한 기억이 지금 여기서
우리가 맞닥뜨리는 현재와는 무관하다고 여기기에 생겨난다. 하지만 지금 우리가
목격하고 있는 중요한 국제적 사건은, 우리가 기억하는 건 과거의 것이지만 그를
기억하는 행위는 늘 현재적이라는 사실을 알려준다. 우크라이나 침공을 위해 러시아
대통령 푸틴이 내세운 첫 번째 명분은 우크라이나를 "나치로부터 해방시킨다"(Ent-
nazifisierung)는 것이다. 주권국인 우크라이나에 군대를 진격시키는 일에 이런 명분이
제기될 수 있었던 이유는 무엇일까? 제2차 세계대전 말 베를린을 점령함으로써
결정적으로 나치 정권을 끝장낼 수 있었던 과거 구소련의 기억 덕분이다. 1945년 5월,
전세계를 나치에게 해방시켰던 소비에트사회주의공화국연방의 '영광스러운' 과거가
2022년 2월, 러시아 군대를 우크라이나에 진입시키는 명분으로 소환된 것이다. 참전한
러시아 군인들이 러시아 정부로부터 들은 건, 나치 지배하에 신음하는 우크라이나
시민들로부터 열렬한 환영을 받을 것이라는 거짓 선전이었다. 이러한 러시아의 침공에
맞서 결연하게 싸우고 있는 우크라이나 역시 과거의 기억을 소환한다. 우크라이나
대통령 볼로디미르 젤렌스키는 텔레그램이나 트위터를 통한 대국민 메시지에서
2014년 러시아의 크림반도 점령을, 같은 해 우크라이나의 민주화 투쟁—이에 대해선
넷플릭스 다큐멘터리 「Winter on Fire」를 보라—에 대한 기억들을 상기시킨다. 지금
이 시간에도 진행 중인 러시아와 우크라이나의 전장에서 서로 맞부닥치고 있는 건 두
나라의 군사력만이 아니다. 현재의 투쟁 속에는 두 나라가 연루된 과거와 그에 대한
기억이 함께 징집되어 싸우고 있다.

발터 벤야민은 이렇게 현재로 소환되는 과거의 기억에 대해
"회억"(Eingedenken)이라는 개념으로 논한 바 있다.[1] 회억은 과거가 당면한 현재의
문제와 실천적으로 결합되면서 상기되는 일을 가리킨다. 회억 속에서 지나간 과거는
그 당시의 흐름과 맥락으로부터 절단되어 수십 년, 아니 수백 년의 시간적 거리를
단숨에 훌쩍 뛰어넘어 "호랑이의 도약처럼" 지금의 시간 속으로 엄습해 들어온다.
우리의 현재는 과거에 대한 기억을 통해 자신을 정당화한다. 현재란, 과거의 영광을

[1]
이에 대해선 김남시, 「과거를
어떻게 (대)할 것인가: 발터
벤야민의 회억 개념」, 『안과밖』,
37권(2014), 243-272 참조.

[1]
For more on this, see Kim Namsee, "How to Handle the past: The Concept of "Eingedenken" by Walter Benjamin," *In/Outside*, no. 37 (2014), 243–272.

Memory: just some vain pursuit, humble and abject, for people with nothing to preoccupy themselves in the present and nothing better to do than to long for bygone things or indulge in self-pitying regrets, or perhaps to boast of past glories? Is reminiscence some leisurely, unproductive pastime, where we turn our backs on a more important and pressing present to concern ourselves with the past? Such questions arise from our view of memories of past things as being unrelated to the present we are confronted with here and now. But the major international incident that we are witnessing today shows us that while the things we remember belong to the past, the act of remembering is always in the present tense. The first pretext that Russian President Vladimir Putin offered for invading Ukraine was the country's "de-Nazification." What factor allowed this to serve as a rationale for attacking the army of a sovereign state like Ukraine? It was the memory of Soviet Russia's ability to decisively put an end to the Nazi government in Germany through its occupation of Berlin at the end of World War II. This glorious past of the Soviet Union, with its liberation of the world from the Nazis in May 1945, was invoked once again in February 2022 as a pretext for sending Russian troops into Ukraine. The Russian soldiers taking part in the invasion heard false propaganda from their government, which told them they would be welcomed with open arms by Ukrainians suffering under Nazi rule. Ukraine, for its part, has also drawn on memories of the past in its resolute battle against the Russian invasion. In his messages to the Ukrainian people, President Volodymyr Zelensky appeals to memories of Russia's occupation of the Crimean Peninsula in 2014 and the democracy struggle in Ukraine the same year (for more on this, see the Netflix documentary *Winter on Fire*). It is not only the two countries' military capabilities that are clashing in the battle that continues to rage between Russia and Ukraine at this moment. Also being mustered in the present struggle are the two countries' pasts and the memories associated with them.

Walter Benjamin used the concept of "Eingedenken" (remembrance) to discuss these sorts of past memories that are invoked in the present.[1] Eingedenken refers to a process in which the past is recalled in a way that is associated in a real way with present-day issues. In Eingedenken, the past becomes disassociated from its contemporary currents and context, crossing decades, if not centuries, of temporal distance to spring into the present time like a "tiger's leap." Our present today justifies itself through memories of the past. The present is a place that roils with the desire to restore past glories or to overcome past humiliations, with the wish to achieve what should have happened before or to avenge past injustices. Memories of the past are forever being recalled through these forces, mustered and mobilized, as they seek in their own ways to assign meaning and direction to the present. Individuals are no

되살리거나 과거의 비루함을 넘어서려는 바램으로, 그때 일어났어야 했으나 그러지 못했던 것을 실현하거나 과거의 부당함을 앙갚음하고자 하는 욕망으로 부글거리는 장소이기 때문이다. 과거에 대한 기억은 각자의 방식으로 현재를 의미화하고 방향성을 부여하려는 이 모든 힘들에 의해 끊임없이 소환되고, 징집되며, 동원된다. 과거의 기억이 현재와 함께 만들어내는 이 복잡한 연루 관계는 개인에게도 예외가 아니다. 우리 한 명 한 명의 개인들은 스스로 의식하지 못하는 사이에 더 깊은 층위에서 기억에 의해 규정 받고 영향을 받는다. 기회가 있을 때마다 현재화되는 기억은 지금의 삶에 막강한 영향을 미친다. 날카롭게 떠오르는 좌절과 실패에 대한 기억은 현재를 살아가고 있는 나의 힘과 에너지를 순식간에 빼앗아버리기도 하고, 어떤 기억은 현재의 좌절과 실패로부터 벗어나는데 도움을 주기도 한다. 지금의 내가 나 자신을 어떻게 정의하고 있는가가 지금 자신의 과거를 어떻게 기억하고 있는가에 따라 달라진다는 건 주지의 사실이다. 현재의 자신을 나름의 성공과 성취라고 긍정하는 사람에게는 과거의 고통과 불행에 대한 기억은 그를 극복하고 이겨낸 현재에 대한 만족과 자신감을 마련해주는 요인으로 작용하는 반면, 자신의 현재를 고통스러운 실패와 좌절의 상태라 여기는 사람에게 과거는 현재의 초라함을 부각하는 영광스러운 누더기로 기억된다. 이렇게 작용하며 그 힘을 발휘하고 있는 기억은 때때로 추억에 빠져들기 위해 들추어보는 사진 앨범 같은 것을 넘어선다. 기억은 지금의 우리가 자기 자신에 대해 가지고 있는 자기감, 정체성을 규정하는 살아있는 힘으로 작동한다. 지나간 시간에 대한 기억은 우리가 살아가는 지금, 현재 속에서 함께 꿈틀거리며 우리의 현재를 지배한다. 우리의 현재는 과거에 대한 우리의 기억에 물들어있다.

미술은 매우 오래전부터 기억을 다루어왔다. 아니 미술의 역사 자체가 기억을 위해 존재해왔다고 말해도 과언이 아니다. 서양 미술의 기원에 대해 말할라치면 빠짐없이 등장하는 고대 이집트 파이윰 초상화는 죽은 자의 미라 위에 사실적이고 생생하게 고인의 얼굴을 그려 놓은 그림이다. 죽은 자의 영혼이 자신의 시신을 알아보기 위해, 살아남은 자가 죽은 자를 기억하기 위해서였다. 같은 이유에서 고대 로마 납골당에는 죽은 자의 흉상이 함께 배치되어 있었다. 왕이나 황제 같은 지배자들은 살아있을 때는 물론 죽은 후에도 자신의 영광스러운 승리와 지배에 대한 기억이 유지되기 위해 주화에, 건물 벽에 거대하게 자신들의 모습을 새겨 넣게 했다. 인류 문명 초창기부터 존재한 주술과 종교는 사람들로 하여금 자신들이 섬기는 신들과 그들이 일구어낸 기적과 일화를 기억하기 위해 건축물과 벽화, 수많은 조각과 그림들을 만들게 하였다. 이를 미술의 역사적 기원이라 부를 수 있다면, 미술은 그 기원에서부터 기억에 대한 요구에서 생겨났다고 말할 수 있다. 종교와 황제의 시대가 지나고 시민들의 힘이 강해졌을 때에도 미술은 기억의 중요한 담지자 역할을 했다. 예를 들어 서양 미술사 최초의 독립된 조각품으로 알려진 도나텔로의 〈다비드상〉은 경쟁 도시국가 밀라노와의 전쟁에서 성취한 영광스러운 승리를 온 시민이 기억하기 위해 광장에 세워진 공공미술이었다. 피카소의 〈게르니카〉는 스페인 내전 시기 비행기 폭격으로 한 마을 주민들을 학살했던 나치의 과거를 기억하기 위해, 케테 콜비츠의

exception to the complex entanglements that past memories create in conjunction with the present. Without our conscious awareness, we as individuals are being defined and influenced by memory at our deeper levels. Transported to the present at every opportunity, memories exert an immense influence on our lives today. Piercing memories of frustration and failure may suddenly rob us of our strength and energy today; conversely, some memories may help us overcome the frustration and failure we are now experiencing. It is widely acknowledged that how we define ourselves now depends on how we remember our own past. For those who affirm themselves as successful and accomplished in their own way, memories of past suffering and misfortune serve to provide a sense of satisfaction and confidence with a present where we have triumphed over them. For those who regard their present as a state of agonizing failure and frustration, the past is remembered as glories in tatters, underscoring their sorry lot today. Exerting its power in these ways, memory is more than just a photo album that we flip through from time to time to immerse ourselves in the past. It operates as a living force that defines the identity and sense of self that we possess today. Memories of past times govern our present, living and breathing within the current moment that we are experiencing. Our present is colored by our memories of the past.

Art has been dealing with memory since time immemorial. Indeed, it would not be overstating things to say that the history of art itself has existed for the sake of memory. The Fayum mummy portraits of ancient Egypt, which are invariably mentioned in any discussion of the origins of Western art, were vivid, realistic images painted on mummies to show the face of the deceased. They were intended so that the soul of the departed would recognize their own body, and so that the living could remember the dead. For the same reason, busts of the deceased were placed in the crypts of ancient Rome. Kings, emperors, and other rulers had images of themselves emblazoned on coins and building walls so that memories of their illustrious victories and dominance would be preserved not only while they were alive but also after their death. Occult practices and religions, present since the dawn of human civilization, instructed people to create structures, murals, and countless sculptures and paintings to remember the deities they served, the stories associated with them, and the miracles they performed. If this can be described as the historical origin of art, then we can say that art emerged from the outset out of a demand for remembrance. Even as the age of religion and emperors passed and the public grew in strength, art continued to play a key role as a bearer of memory. For instance, Donatello's *David*, which is recognized as the first standalone sculpture in Western art history, was a work of public art erected in a public square so that everyone would remember the glorious victory achieved by Florence in its battle with rival city-state Milan. Pablo Picasso's *Guernica* was meant to remember the past deeds of the Nazis, who massacred an entire village in an air raid during the Spanish Civil War. *Mother with Her Dead Son* by Käthe Kollwitz remembers those who have been forced into wars and sacrificed to dictatorships. *The Great East World* and *The Parade of the March* by Hong Sungdam remember the vitality of the masses who rose up against the massacre perpetrated by the South Korean military government in Gwangju. In short, the history of art is a product of human actions meant to hold on to memories of events that might otherwise vanish with the passage of time.

The things that we strive to remember in this way are things that cannot exist anywhere except in memory. The things we seek to remember are not the principles of the cosmos

[2]
발터 벤야민, 『일방통행로/
사유이미지』, 최성만 외
옮김(서울: 도서출판 길, 2007).

〈피에타〉는 전쟁에 내몰리고 독재에 희생된 사람들을 기억하기 위해, 홍성담 작가의
〈대동세상〉이나 〈횃불행진〉은 군부에 의한 광주학살에 맞서 일어선 민중들의 생명력을
기억하기 위한 것이다. 한마디로 미술의 역사는 시간이 지나면 사라져버리는 사건들의
기억을 담지하려는 인간 행위의 산물이었다.

　　우리가 이렇게 기억하고자 애쓰는 것들은, 기억이 아니면 그 어디에도 존재할
수 없는 것들이다. 우리가 기억하려는 건 우주와 생명체의 원리들이 아니다. 그런
것이라면 우리가 따로 기억하지 않아도 이미 우주의 만물과 생명체들 속에 새겨져
확고하게 존재한다. 학문과 과학은 우주와 생명체에 새겨진 것들을 연구하며 지금까지
상당한 것들을 밝혀내었다. 시간이 지날수록 우리는 그에 대해 더 많은 것을 알게 될
것이다. 우리가 기억하려는 것들은 이와는 사정이 다르다. 그것은 이곳에서 일어났던
일, 한때 여기 살았던 사람들, 그들이 살아있는 동안 행한 일들이다. 이들은 어딘가에
물질적, 물리적으로 새겨져 있지 않기에 시간 앞에 극도로 취약하다. 이들은 그때, 그
시간이 지나면 별다른 흔적 없이 사라지고 시간 속에서 소멸한다. 한때 그러했던 것,
언젠가 거기 있었던 것, 여기 살았었기에 죽은 자들, 이들은 시간이 지날수록 점점
늘어나지만—그래서 벤야민은 "죽은 자들의 세계는 늘 산 자들의 그것보다 크다"고
말한다[2]—그렇게 시간이 지날수록 발견되기보다는 사라져버리기 십상이다. 우리가
멈출 수도, 되돌릴 수도 없는 시간 속에서 사라져 가는 것들, 시간 앞에서 스스로
자신의 존속을 유지할 수 없는 이 취약한 것들에 대해 우리가 할 수 있는 최대치가
기억이다. 그들에 대해서 우리는 기억하는 것 말고는 달리 할 수 있는 게 없기
때문이다.

　　그런데 이렇게만 말하면 기억이란 기억하려는 의지와 선택에 달려있는 것인 양
오해할 수도 있겠다. 전혀 그렇지 않다는 건 우리 모두가 알고 있다. 우리는, 기억하고
싶지만 망각되는 것들과 망각하고 싶으나 불쑥 불쑥 솟구쳐 오르는 기억들로 시름에
빠진다. 많은 경우 기억은 우리의 의식적 선택이나 의지를 훌쩍 벗어나 있다. 20세기
초 생물학과 정신분석 이론은 기억이 의식과는 독립적으로, 심지어 개인적 차원을
넘어 작동한다는 사실을 다양한 정황증거들을 통해 밝혔다. 프로이트는 우리가 태어난
후부터 맞닥뜨리는 어떤 사건들은 우리의 의식적 표상을 거치지 않는다는 걸, 다시
말해 우리가 전혀 알지 못한 채 기억된다는 사실을 밝혔다. 그렇게 자리 잡은 무의식적
기억은 자아 정체성의 발달에 심대한 영향을 미치며, 어떤 경우엔 증상과 병의 원인이
되기도 한다. 프로이트는 「토템과 터부」, 「문화와 그 불만」 등 논고를 통해 인간이
개체적으로 경험할 수 없었던, 어떤 근원적인 유적 기억이 현재 우리의 삶에 함께
작동하고 있다는 가설을 내세우기도 하였다.

　　생물학자들은 뇌 같은 중추기관을 가지지 않는 단세포 생물들, 그렇기에 의식도,
지각을 통한 표상도 없는 생물들이 일정한 형태와 구조를 만들어내며 섭식과 번식을
행하는 걸 관찰하였다. 이는 의식에 의존하지 않는 종류의 기억이, 뇌가 아닌 세포에,
신체에 존재하는 기억이 작동하고 있음을 말해준다. 1870년 신경생리학자 에발트
헤링은 「조직된 물질의 일반적 기능으로서 기억에 대하여」(Über das Gedächtnis als
allgemeine Funktion der organisierten Materie)라는 저술을 통해 기억이 "조직된

[2]
Walter Benjamin, "One-Way
Street" in *One-Way Street/
Thought-Images*, trans. Choi
Seong Man (Seoul: Gil, 2007).

and organisms. If they were, they would exist robustly within the phenomena and life of the universe without our having to remember them. Scholars and scientists have discovered many things in their studies of the things engraved in the universe and life. In the fullness of time, we will learn even more about them. It is a different situation with the things we attempt to remember: the events that happened in a particular place, the people who once lived there, the things they did while they were alive. These are not inscribed in any material or physical way, which makes them exceedingly vulnerable to time. Once their moment passes, they disappear more or less without a trace, fading away into history. Over time, these things proliferate: the way things were at a particular time, the things that existed there at some point, the people who died because they lived there; this is why Benjamin spoke of the world of the dead as always being larger than the world of the living.[2] But as time goes by, they are more likely to vanish than to be discovered. Memory is the most that we can do for those things that vanish into the unstopped, irreversible flow of time, those vulnerable things that cannot sustain themselves in the face of time. There is nothing else we can do for them except to remember them.

But to speak of things solely in these terms could lead to the misunderstanding that memory depends on the will and decision to remember. As we all know, this is by no means the case. All of us struggle with the things that end up forgotten despite our wish to remember them, as well as the memories that we would like to forget but that keep popping up unbidden. In many instances, memory is a matter far beyond any conscious decision or will on our part. During the early 20th century, biology and psychoanalytical theory discovered various circumstantial evidence showing that memory operates independently from consciousness—even beyond the personal level. Sigmund Freud showed that some of the events that we encounter from the time we are born do not pass through any conscious representation within us; in other words, they are remembered without our being aware of them at all. Once established, these unconscious memories have a profound influence on the development of our self-identity. In some cases, they may be the cause of symptoms and diseases. Freud also hypothesized that some primal historical memories—things that we human beings could not have individually experienced—continue to operate in our lives today in *Totem and Taboo* and *Civilization and Its Discontents.*

Biologists have observed how single-celled organisms without brains or similar vital organs—and thus without consciousness or perception-based representations— establish certain forms and structures as they feed and procreate. This indicates the workings of the sort of memory that does not rely on consciousness, and that exists in the cells of the body rather than the brain. In 1870, the neurophysiologist Ewald Hering argued in his "Über das Gedächtnis als allgemeine Funktion der organisierten Materie" (On Memory as a General Function of Organized Matter) that memory was a "function of organized matter." Memories, he claimed, were transmitted to the next generation not through consciousness but through the organism's neural substances, ensuring that individuals of the same species would be able to metabolize and reproduce in the same way. It is thanks to these inherited memories that a newly born organism is able to begin carrying out the movements necessary for its immediate survival, without any learning process based on perceptual experience and consciousness. Hering's argument was carried on by the evolutionary biologist Richard Semon, who claimed that the things

물질의 기능"임을 주장하였다. 기억은 의식이 아니라 생명체의 신경 물질을 통해 다음 세대 개체에게 유전되며, 그에 의해 동일종의 생명체가 같은 방식의 신진대사와 재생산을 할 수 있게 보장한다는 것이다. 이제 막 탄생한 생명체가 지각경험과 의식을 통한 학습 과정 없이도 즉각 생존에 필수적인 운동을 시작할 수 있는 건 이렇게 전달되는 기억 덕분이다. 헤링의 주장을 계승한 진화생물학자 리하르트 볼프강 제몬은 살아있는 동안 생물에게 일어나는 사건들은 "엔그램"(Engramm)이라 불리는 생물의 물질에 그 흔적을 남기며, 여기 보존되던 에너지 잠재성이 적절한 조건 하에서 다시 활성화되고 방전되어 나온다고 주장했다. 기억은 의식의 내용이 아니라, 생명체를 구성하는 신경물질에 저장되어 다음 세대로 유전되기도 하는 잠재적 에너지라는 것이다.[3]

비슷한 시기인 1872년 찰스 다윈은 『인간과 동물의 감정표현』(The Expression of the Emotions in Man and Animals)에서 동물과 인간의 무의지적 표정이나 몸짓을, 개체를 넘어서는 종적 기억의 산물로 이해할 길을 열어주었다. 다윈의 핵심 가설은 분노, 경악, 경계, 유쾌함과 슬픔 등 특정 상황에서 즉각적으로 드러나는 동물과 인간의 감정표현이 초기 진화단계에서 의지적으로 수행한 행동의 무의식적 기억이라는 것이다.

"아득히 먼 옛날에 의식적으로 행해졌던 일부 행동들은 습관, 그리고 연계를 통해 반사작용으로 전환되었으며, 이들은 현재 매우 확고하게 우리에게 고정되어 유전되고 있다. 이에 따라 아주 먼 옛날에 의지에 의해 행해졌던 행동을 촉발했던 동일한 원인이 오늘날의 인류에게 작용하게 되면, 설령 별다른 도움이 되지 않을지라도, 사람들이 그와 같은 행동을 하게 되는 것이다."[4]

공포, 불안, 슬픔, 경악 등의 내적 감정을 불러내는 상황 속에서 의식하지 못하는 사이에 움직이는 우리의 신체 근육들은 '아득히 먼 옛날' 어떤 기능과 유용성을 지니고 있던 의식적 움직임의 기억을 간직하고 있다. 특정 상황에 특정한 몸짓과 표정으로 반응하는 우리 신체에는 먼 과거의 신체적 기억이 작동하고 있다는 것이다. 이런 신체적 기억은 의식의 내용으로 존재하지 않는다. 그건 특정한 감정을 느낄 때 특정한 방식의 신체 움직임을 촉발하고, 특정한 신체적 표현을 마주할 때 우리에게 있는 내적 감정을 활성화시키는 살아 움직이는 에너지처럼 작동한다. 이러한 신체적 기억은 누군가의 특정한 표정과 몸짓을 접하는 우리에게 그와 신체적으로 결부되어 있는 내적 감정을 활성화시키는 방식으로도 작동한다.[5] 이렇게 작동하는 신체적 기억에 대한 이해에 입각해 아비 바르부르크는 분노, 고통, 공포와 같은 상황에서 생겨나는 신체 이미지와 상징들이 예술 작품을 시간과 지역을 넘어서는 근원적인 기억의 매개체로 작동할 수 있다고 생각하였다.[6]

'의식을 매개하지 않는 기억, 지각적 표상을 매개하지 않고 우리 신체 어딘가에 저장되어 있는 기억. 의식되지는 못하지만 지각하고, 말하고, 느끼고 반응하는 우리의

[3]
Ernst H. Gobrich, *Aby Warburg: Eine intellektuelle Biografie* (Hamburg: Europäische Verlagsanstalt, 1992), 325–326.

[4]
찰스 다윈, 『인간과 동물의 감정표현』, 김성한 옮김 (서울: 사이언스북스, 2020), 90.

[5]
신경과학자들은 인간이 특정행위를 할 때 활성화되는 뇌세포가 타인의 그 행위를 보기만 해도 활성화된다는 사실을 발견하고 이를 '거울뉴런'이라 불렀다. 타인의 특정한 표정과 몸짓을 보는 것만으로 우리 두뇌의 운동피질을 자극해 부지불식간에 우리 자신에게도 같은 표정과 몸짓을 유발하는 'emotional contagion'도 증명되었다. David A. Freedberg, "Feelings on Faces from Physiognomy to Neuroscience," in *Rethinking Emotion: Interiority and Exteriority, Premodern, Modern, and Contemporary Thought*, ed. Rüdiger Campe, Julia Weber (Berlin: De Gruyter, 2014) 참조.

[6]
이에 대해선 김남시, 「잔존하는 이미지의 힘. 아비 바르부르크의 역동적 이미지론」, 『현대미술학 논문집』, 23권, 2호(2019), 85–111 참조.

[3]
Ernst H. Gobrich, *Aby Warburg: Eine intellektuelle Biografie* (Hamburg: Europäische Verlagsanstalt, 1992), 325–326.

[4]
Charles Darwin, *The Expression of the Emotions in Man and Animals* (New York: D. Appleton & Company, 1897), 39–40.

[5]
Neuroscientists have discovered that certain neurons activated when a human being performs a particular action are also activated when they see others perform the same action; these cells have been referred to as "mirror neurons." They have also demonstrated what is known as "emotional contagion," where the mere sight of another person's expression and gesture can stimulate our brain's motor cortex to unwittingly induce the same expression and gesture in us. See David A. Freedberg, "Feelings on Faces from Physiognomy to Neuroscience," in *Rethinking Emotion: Interiority and Exteriority, Premodern, Modern, and Contemporary Thought*, ed. Rüdiger Campe, Julia Weber (Berlin: De Gruyter, 2014).

[6]
For more on this, see Kim Namsee, "Nachleben of Image. Aby Warburg's theory of visual image," *Journal of Contemporary Art Studies,* vol. 23, no. 2 (2019), 85–111.

that happen to a living organism leave an imprint called an "engram" on its physical substance, preserved as energy potentiality that is reactivated and discharged under the appropriate conditions. Memory, in other words, is not the content of consciousness, but potential energy that is stored in the organism's neural substances and passed on to the next generation.[3]

Around the same time, Charles Darwin wrote his 1872 work *The Expression of the Emotions in Man and Animals*, which paved the way for the understanding of the nonvolitional expressions and movements of animals and human beings as the product of species-based memories transcending the individual. Darwin's key hypothesis was that human and animal expressions of emotions that appear spontaneously in certain situations—such as anger, surprise, alarm, pleasure, and sadness—represent unconscious memories of actions performed volitionally at earlier stages of evolution:

> "From the foregoing remarks it seems probable that some actions, which were at first performed consciously, have become through habit and association converted into reflex actions, and are now so firmly fixed and inherited, that they are performed, even when not of the least use, as often as the same causes arise, which originally excited them in us through the volition." [4]

Operating unconscious in situations that evoke internal emotions such as fear, anxiety, sadness, or surprise, the muscles of our body harbor memories of consciousness movements that "at first" held some function and utility. In other words, physical memories from the distant past operate in our bodies as they react to certain situations with specific movements and expressions. Such physical memories do not exist as the content of our consciousness. They act as living energy, inciting particular movements of the body when we experience particular emotions and activating the emotions within us when we are faced with particular physical expressions. These physical memories also function to activate the physically associated internal emotions when we encounter particular expressions and gestures in others.[5] Based on this understanding of the workings of physical memory, Aby Warburg thought that the physical images and symbols that arise in situations such as anger, pain, and fear could transform art into a medium of primordial memory transcending time and region.[6]

Memories that are not mediated by consciousness; memories stored somewhere in our body without passing through perceptual representation; memories that are constantly, unconsciously operating on our present moment as we perceive, speak, feel, and react—such memories cannot be entirely summoned or expressed through "representation." The representation that art has used since time immemorial to address memory has chiefly entailed recording the object to be remembered in non-moving visual images such as painting or sculpture, invoking the object that is mediated through visual perception of the image. Memory in this case is borne by consciousness, which is capable of recalling a certain entity, and that recollection process typically operates at a cognitive level. Marcel, the protagonist in *In Search of Lost Time*, do not offer a representative example of a character illustrating how our attempts to remember at a cognitive level may succeed in recalling the important things, after straining to remember something valuable about Combray, the town where he once lived, he finally reaches the following conclusion: "And so it is with our own past. It is a labour in vain

현재에 끊임없이 작용하고 있는 기억. 이러한 신체적 기억은 '재현'의 방식만으로 불러내거나 표현되기는 어렵다. 오래전부터 미술이 기억을 다루는 것에 활용해왔던 재현은 주로, 그림이나 조각 등 움직이지 않는 시각적 이미지로 기억하려는 대상을 기록하고, 그 이미지에 대한 시각적 지각을 매개해 그 대상에 대한 표상을 불러낸다. 여기서 기억은 어떤 표상을 떠올릴 수 있는 의식에 의해 담지되고 그런 회상의 과정은 주로 인지적 차원에서 작동한다. 『잃어버린 시간을 찾아서』의 주인공 마르셀은 인지적 층위에서 이루어지는 기억에의 시도가 정작 중요한 것을 상기하는데 그리 큰 효과를 불러내지 못한다는 걸 보여준 대표적인 인물일 것이다. 그는 한동안 자신이 살았던 콩브레에 대해 무언가 값진 것을 떠올리려고 애쓰다가 결국 이런 결론을 내린다. "우리의 과거를 불러오려고 아무리 시도해도, 우리의 정신은 헛되이 애쓸 뿐이다. 과거는 정신의 힘이 미치는 영역 바깥에 있으며 정신으로서는 알 수 없는 어떤 물질적인 대상(혹은 이 대상이 우리에게 일깨우는 느낌) 속에 숨겨져 있다. 그렇지만 그것이 어떤 대상인지 우리는 알 수 없다. 우리가 이 대상을 죽기 전에 접할 수 있을지, 아니면 결코 만나지 못할지 전적으로 우연에 달려있다."[7]

아무리 의식적으로 노력해도 불러내어지지 않는 과거를 결국 '잃어버린 시간'이라며 거의 포기해 가던 어느 날, 경이롭게 그 기억을 되살려 준 건 무척이나 사소하게 보이는 한 감각적, 신체적 경험이었다. "나는 막막한 날과 우울한 날들이 이어질 것에 대한 예감에 짓눌린 채 차 한 스푼에 마들렌 조각을 적셔 입에 가져갔다. 케이크 맛과 섞인 한 모금의 차가 내 잇몸에 닿는 순간 내 몸은 움찔했으며 무엇인가 내 속에서 일상적이지 않은 것이 일어난 듯했다. 오로지 나만을 위해 존재하고 그 이유를 내가 알 수 없는, 지금껏 한 번도 겪어본 적 없던 행복한 감정이 나를 관통해 흘렀다. 단 한 번에 내게 삶의 번잡한 일들이 그리 대수롭지 않은 것으로, 삶의 파국이란 게 별거 아닌 불운으로, 삶의 단명함이란 감각의 기만에 다름 아닌 것이 되어버렸다. 사랑만이 줄 수 있었던 어떤 것이 내 속에서 일어났고, 나는 지극히 값진 실체가 나를 꽉 채우고 있는 느낌을 받았다. 아니 그 실체가 내 속에 있는 게 아니라 나 자신이 그 실체가 된 느낌이었다. 나 자신이 별 볼 일 없고, 우연적이며 죽을 수밖에 없는 존재라는 느낌이 사라졌다."[8]

의식적으로 떠올리려면 아무리 해도 불러내어지지 않지만, "내 정신을 분산시키고, 다른 것을 생각하고 동시에 휴식을 취할 때"[9] 다시 말해 "현재적 행동으로부터 초연해지고, 무용한 것에 가치를 부여하며, 꿈꾸려는"[10] 순간 비로소 "꿈틀거리며 솟아오르는" 이러한 기억을 프루스트는 "무의지적 기억"(la mémoire involontaire)이라 불렀다. 잠을 자거나 몽상에 젖을 때 일어나는 이러한 기억을 베르그송은 '행위하는 인간'의 목적지향성에 도움을 주는 정상적 기억의 기능으로부터의 일탈이자, 올바른 행위를 가로막는 장애 혹은 병리적 증상으로 본 반면,[11] 작가인 프루스트는 잠재적으로 숨어있고, 의지로서 호출할 수 없고, 예견과 컨트롤이 불가능한 자극과 만나 비로소 생생하게 떠오르는 이러한 기억을 그 기억을 불러내기 위한 주체적 상태, 곧 "어떠한 의식적 노력도 없고, 어떠한 지성의 개입도

[7]
Marcel Proust, *In Swanns Welt. Auf der Suche nach der verlorenen Zeit*, Erster Teil (Berlin: Shurkamp,1981), 63.

[8]
Ibid., 63-64

[9]
Ibid., 65.

[10]
앙리 베르그송, 『물질과 기억』, 박종원 옮김(서울: 아카넷, 2005), 144.

[11]
L.A. Bisson, "Proust, Bergson and George Elito," *The Modern Language Review,* vol. 40, no. 2 (1945), 107.

[7]
Marcel Proust, *Swann's Way*, trans. C. K. Scott Moncrieff, Terence Kilmartin (New York: Random House, 1992), 60.

[8]
Ibid., 60–61.

[9]
Ibid., 62.

[10]
Henri Bergson, *Matter and Memory*, trans. Park Jongwon (Seoul: Acanet, 2005), 144.

[11]
L.A. Bisson, "Proust, Bergson and George Eliot," *The Modern Language Review*, vol. 40, no. 2 (Apr. 1945), 107.

[12]
Ibid., 108.

to attempt to recapture it: all the efforts of our intellect must prove futile. The past is hidden somewhere outside the realm, beyond the reach of intellect, in some material object (in the sensation which that material object will give us) of which we have no inkling. And it depends on chance whether or not we come upon this object before we ourselves must die." [7]

Just as Marcel was abandoning the past as "lost time" that he could never summon back no matter how hard he consciously tried, the memory was miraculous recalled by a seemingly trivial physical and sensory experience: "...mechanically, dispirited after a dreary day with the prospect of a depressing morrow, I raised to my lips a spoonful of the tea in which I had soaked a morsel of the cake. No sooner had the warm liquid mixed with the crumbs touched my palate than a shiver ran through me and I stopped, intent upon the extraordinary thing that was happening to me. An exquisite pleasure had invaded my senses, something isolated, detached, with no suggestion of its origin. And at once the vicissitudes of life had become indifferent to me, its disasters innocuous, its brevity illusory—this new sensation having had the effect, which love has, of filling me with a precious essence; or rather than this essence was not in me, it was me. I had ceased now to feel mediocre, contingent, mortal." [8]

Proust used the term la mémoire involontaire—"involuntary memory"—to describe the kind of memory that does not come to us when we attempt to consciously recall it, but that "starts within" us when we "enjoy a distraction" rest as we think of other things [9]—in other words, when we "attempt to dream, becoming detached from present actions and assigning value to pointless things." [10] This sort of memory that arises when we are sleeping or daydreaming was seen by Bergson as a deviation from the normal functioning of memory, which aids the goal-directed behaviors of the "acting human being," and as a kind of disorder or pathological symptoms preventing proper behavior. [11]

In contrast, the writer Proust viewed such memories—concealed in potential form, unable to be summoned at will, but coming to vivid life when we encounter some unpredictable and uncontrollable stimulus—as being a key condition for artistic creation, alongside the subjective state that seeks to evoke them, the state of receptiveness without any conscious effort or involvement of the intellect. [12]

The method of representation based on conscious symbolization is not enough to evoke the mémoires involontaires that are stored unconsciously somewhere in the body to be transmitted and expressed through physical perceptions. Walter Benjamin saw a departure from self-consciousness as an essential condition for these sorts of memories to be evoked—something he referred to as "mental relaxation" or "self-forgetting" ("The Storyteller") or as "existing outside of oneself" ("A Berlin Chronicle," "Moscow Diary"). The artworks presented in the National Museum of Modern and Contemporary Art, Korea exhibition *My Your Memory* represent a wide range of media and genre, including painting, Mixografia, installation, and video. They can be related to memories in some form at various levels, yet they exist beyond the approach of representing past events and individuals. What is noteworthy about these works is how memories activate memories mediated through the body in various ways.

Sleep by Andy Warhol could hardly be described as a mere "representation" of the artist's lover John Giorno sleeping. The very length of the work, which continues for five hours and twenty-one minutes, creates a kind of surplus situation that vastly

없는 수용성의 상태"와 더불어 작품 창작의 핵심 조건으로 삼았다.[12]

[12]
Ibid., 108.

의식에 의한 표상을 기반으로 하는 '재현'의 방식은, 이렇게 무의식적으로, 신체 어딘가에 저장되고 신체적 감각을 통해 전달되며 표현되는 '무의지적 기억'을 불러내기에 충분하지 못하다. 발터 벤야민은 이러한 종류의 기억이 소환되기에 필수불가결한 조건을 자기의식에서 벗어나는 탈자아적 태도라고 보고 이를 "정신적 이완", "자기망각"(「이야기꾼」), "우리 자신의 바깥에 있음"(「베를린 연대기」, 「모스크바 일기」)라는 표현으로 지칭하였다. 이번 국립현대미술관의 《나너의 기억》 전에 소개된 작품들은 회화, 믹소그라피, 설치, 영상 등 다양한 매체와 장르를 망라한다. 여기 전시된 작품들은 여러 층위에서 어떤 식으로든 기억과 관련시켜 볼 수 있으면서도 과거의 사건이나 인물을 재현하는 방식에서 벗어나있다. 이 작품들에서 기억은 다양한 방식으로 신체를 매개한 기억을 활성화시킨다는 점에서 주목할만하다.

앤디 워홀의 작품 〈수면〉이 워홀의 동성애인 존 지오르노가 자는 모습을 단지 '재현'하고만 있다고 말하기는 힘들다. 5시간 21분에 달하는 이 영상의 길이 자체가 이것이 '무엇에 관한 것'이라는 인지를 크게 초과하는 어떤 잉여를 만들어내고 있기 때문이다. 우리가 보고 있는 게 무엇인지 알아보기 힘들 정도로 클로즈업된 지오르노의의 가슴, 엉덩이, 입술과 얼굴은 흑백 필름 카메라 특유의 기계적 리듬과 결합되어 다다의 실험영화처럼 추상적이다. 그렇기에 이 작품에 기록된 것은 '자고 있는 존 지오르노의'라기 보다는, 손에 카메라를 들고 수면의 호흡에 따라 천천히 오르내리는 애인의 벌거벗은 신체를 이렇게 오랫동안 바라보고 있는 워홀의 욕망/애정이다.

양정욱 작가의 키네틱 작품 〈피곤은 언제나 꿈과 함께〉에서는 중심을 향해 원추형으로 모여 있는 긴 나무 막대들이, 잠자는 존 지오르노의 가슴처럼, 숨을 쉬듯 위 아래로 움직이는 와중에 그에 연결된 코르크 와인 마개 크기의 나무 조각이 실에 매달린 플라스틱 병들을 화들짝 때리며 소리를 낸다. 작가는 아파트 경비실에서 피곤한 경비원이 조는 모습을 보고 이 작품을 만들게 되었다고 말한다. 한 인터뷰에서 작가는 안마 기계를 팔러 다니는 왕년의 안마사, 편의점에서 아르바이트를 하는 과거의 권투 선수, 수신호로 교통을 정리하는 전역 군인의 몸짓에 대해 말한다. 안마 기계를 시연해 보이고, 상품의 바코드를 찍고, 차량의 이동을 지시하는 이들의 신체 움직임에는 과거의 익숙한 몸짓들이 작동하고 있지 않겠냐고 말이다. 작은 모터에 연결된 나무 조각, 실, 철사, 플라스틱 병들이 당장이라도 멈출 듯, 연약하고 어설프게 움직이면서, 의자에 앉은 채 졸다가 화들짝 놀라 고개를 들어 올리는 신체의 움직임을 상기시킨다.

매끈하고 세련된 하이 테크놀로지 시대에 사는 우리들에게 위태롭고 어설프게 작동하는 기계장치들은 '낡아버린 것'의 인상을 불러낸다. 발터 벤야민은, 불과 수년 전만 해도 평범했던 사물을 '낡아버린 것', 과거의 것으로 느끼는 우리의 감성에 부지불식간에 작동하고 있는 집합적 기억에 주목한 바 있다. 끊임없이 새로운 상품을 만들어내는 자본의 순환 관계 속에서 사는 우리에게 '있었던 것'에의 기억은 어느 순간

[13]
Walter Benjamin, *On the Concept of History/On the Critique of Violence /Surrealism*, trans. Choi Seong Man (Seoul: Gil, 2009), 150.

exceeds the time needed to recognize what it is "about." Shown from so close up that it is difficult to discern what we are looking at, Giorno's chest, buttocks, lips, and face combine with the mechanical rhythms of the black-and-white camera to create something as abstract as a Dadaist experimental film. What is thus recorded in the work is less the image of the sleeping John Giorno than the desire/affection that Warhol feels as he holds his camera and gazes for so long at his lover's nude body, rising and falling slowly with his sleeping breaths.

In the kinetic work *Fatigue Always Comes with a Dream* by Yang Junguk, long metal rods converge toward the center in a conical pattern, moving up and down in a breathing motion like the sleeping Giorno's chest. Connected to them is a chunk of wood the size of a wine cork, which is suspended on a string and produces sounds as it raps against the plastic bottles. The artist has said that he created this work after seeing a tired security guard dozing up in an apartment security office. In interviews, he has talked about the movements of former massage therapist peddling massage devices; a former boxer now working part-time in a convenience store; and a discharge soldier using hand signals to direct traffic. As their physical motions demonstrate the devices, scan barcodes, and direct vehicles, the artist questions whether the familiar gestures of the past are at work in them. The wood chunk, thread, wire, and plastic bottles connected to the small motor move in a feeble, halting way, as though they might stop at any moment—recalling the body movements of someone nodding off in a chair, only to raise their head with a start.

For those of us living in an era of sleek and sophisticated high technology, mechanical devices that operate in a precarious, awkward way evoke associations with "obsolescence." Benjamin focused his attention on the collective memories that operate unbeknownst to us in the emotions we experience when we perceive objects that were considered typical just a few years before as now being "obsolete" and part of the past. For those of us who live amid the cyclical relationships of capital that is constantly churning out new items, memories of "what used to be" may transform at some moment into "revolutionary energy." [13] In *Auditorium (Template A–Z)* by Mioon, dozens of low-tech kinetic objects emit bizarre sounds as they project playful yet grotesque shadows like something out of a dream on a screen/wall that surrounds the viewer. The "old-fashioned" devices performing their own noisy movement come together with their shadows to stimulate memories that lay deep within.

Pimple.Blister.Wart.Mole. by Song Joowon consists of the gestures of a performer who recalls memories imbued in a particular places. The film begins with a visit to the Former Armed Forces' Gwangju Hospital, which was once filled with the bodies of citizens injured and killed in the Gwangju Uprising of May 1980. Walking and moving through the dark corridors where those victims lay in the past, the performer uses her body to reenact accounts of the incident at the time. If it is true that ancient memories operate within our gestures—memories that are not even our own alone—then some movements within a setting where certain events occurred may connect the past with the present in practical ways. *My Vietnam Story* by the Chilean poet/artist Cecilia Vicuña uses images to represent the "faint tacit understanding between past and present" formed through these physical memories. In this case, memories of women and children massacred in 1968 during the Vietnam War form a connection to memories of the 1973 military coup that brought Augusto Pinochet to power in Chile, and the resulting deaths.

"혁명적 에너지"[13] 로 전환될 수도 있다. 뮌의 〈오디토리움(Template A-Z)〉은 수십
개의 로우테크 키네틱 오브제들이 기이한 소리를 내며 관객을 둘러싼 스크린 벽에,
꿈 속에서 마주칠 법한 유희스럽고도 그로테스크한 그림자를 만들어낸다. 왁자지껄
제각기 움직이는 '낡은' 기계 장치들과 그들의 그림자가, 깊숙한 곳에 쌓여있던 기억을
자극한다.

송주원 작가의 〈뾰루지.물집.사마귀.점〉은 특정 장소에 서려 있는 기억을 소환하는
퍼포머의 몸짓들로 이루어져 있다. 영상은 5·18 광주민중항쟁 당시 부상당한 시민과
사망자들의 시신들이 가득했던 국군광주병원을 찾아가는 데에서 시작한다. 한때
희생자들이 누워있던 어두운 복도를 걸어가고 움직이면서 그 사건에 대한 진술들을
몸짓으로 되살려낸다. 우리의 몸짓에 아주 오래된, 심지어 나만의 것이 아닌 기억이
작동하고 있는 것이 맞는다면, 과거의 사건들이 벌어진 장소에서 펼쳐지는 어떤
몸짓은 지나간 시대와 지금의 시간을 실천적으로 연결시킬 수 있을 것이다. 칠레의
시인이자 작가인 세실리아 비쿠냐의 〈나의 베트남 이야기〉는 이런 신체적 기억을
통해 맺어지는 "과거와 현재 사이의 희미한 묵계"를 이미지화한다. 여기서는 1968년
베트남전에서 학살당한 여자와 아이들에 대한 기억이 1973년 피노체트 군사 쿠데타와
그 희생자들에 대한 기억과 관계 맺는다. 작품 속에서 이 두 시간을 매개하는 것이,
희생자의 사진을 쓰다듬고, 붉은 스카프를 손목에 차는 작가의 주름진 손이라는 건
의미심장하다.

성급하게 호수에 뛰어들다 바닥에 머리를 찧고 피를 흘리는 모습을 보여줄
뿐인 시프리앙 가이야르 〈호수 아치〉가 보는 이의 몸에 아찔하고 지릿한 감각을
불러내는 건, 이 영상이 우리 신체에서 작동하는 거울뉴런을 자극해 내 스스로 겪지
않았던 과거의 사건을 내 신체의 감각으로 떠올리게 하기 때문일 것이다. 안리
살라는 대사도, 서사도 없는 영상과 사운드만으로 보는 자의 신체감각을 자극하는 데
탁월한 재능을 지닌 작가다. 그의 첫 작품 〈인터뷰(말들을 찾아서)〉(1998)에서부터
현실을 감추고 미화하는 언어의 작용에 회의적이었던 그는, 언어와 같은 의식적,
명시적 기억에 의해 오히려 억압되고, 감추어진 신체의 기억을 활성화시키기 위해
소리와 음악을 사용해왔다. 〈붉은색 없는 1395일〉의 배경은 1992년 4월부터 1395일
동안 세르비아군에게 포위되어 있던 도시 사라예보에서 살아야 했던 시민들의
삶이다. 이 시기 동안 이곳에 살던 시민 1만여 명이 어디선가 날아온 총탄에 목숨을
잃었다. 스나이퍼의 표적이 되기 쉬운 넓은 교차로를 건널 때마다 사람들은 숨을
크게 들이쉬고 목숨을 건 횡단을 감행한다. 교차로 앞에서 자신의 차례를 기다리고,
어디선가 들려오는 총성에 화들짝 놀라면서도 그 잠깐의 틈에 재빨리 내달려야
하는 긴박한 상황의 긴장감이 보는 이의 숨을 죽이게 만든다. 넓은 건널목을 뛰어
건너는 여인의 턱까지 차오르는 급박한 숨소리가 사라예보 관현악단이 연주하는
차이콥스키의 「비창」과 교차하면서 활성화시키는 건, 표상을 통해 떠오르는 이미지가
아닌 신체적 기억이다.

임윤경 작가의 〈Q&A〉나 박혜수 작가의 〈기쁜 우리 젊은 날〉에는 작가의 질문을

[13]
발터 벤야민, 『역사의
개념에 대하여/폭력비판을
위하여/초현실주의 외』, 최성만
옮김(서울: 도서출판 길, 2009),
150.

Significantly, what mediates the two different times in the work is the artist's own wrinkled hand, as it strokes photographs of the victims and wraps a red scarf around her wrist.

The Lake Arches by Cyprien Gaillard merely shows the blood streaming from the head of someone who has dived into a lake without judging the depth and banged his head against the bottom. The reason it evokes feelings of dizziness and excitement in the viewer's body may be because the film stimulates the mirror neurons of our body, evoking past events that we did not ourselves experience as our own physical perceptions. Anri Sala is an artist with an extraordinary gift for eliciting physical sensations in the viewer through image and sound alone, without dialogue or narrative. Skeptical of the ways in which language obscures and whitewashes reality since his first work *Intervista–finding the words* (1998), the artist has used sound and music to activate body memories that have, if anything, been suppressed and hidden by conscious, explicit memories like those associated with language. The backdrop for his *1395 Days Without Red* is the lived experience of citizens who had to survive in Sarajevo when it was under siege by Serbian troops for a 1,395-day period beginning in April 1992. During that time, around 10,000 residents lost their lives to bullets fired from all around. When crossing wide intersections that offer easy targets for snipers, the people take a deep breath before risking their life to get to the other side. They wait their turn at the intersection; when they hear the sound of gunfire somewhere, they are startled, but they must also take advantage of the opportunity to run as fast as they can. The resulting sense of tension is heart-stopping for the viewer. As the urgent breaths of the woman running across the broad crosswalk intersect with a performance of Tchaikovsky's Pathétique symphony by the Sarajevo String Quartet, the result stimulates not images arising through symbolic representation, but rather body memories.

Both *Q&A* by Lim Yoonkyung and *Our Joyful Young Days* by Park Hyesoo feature people recalling past events in response to questions from the artist. At times, these questions stir up memories that lie within us; in such cases, our bodies experience the kind of emotional stirrings that are not present in mechanical recollections resembling memorized answers. *Q&A* features a dialogue between two people who once lived together in the same house, one of them as the owner and the other as a live-in housekeeper. Two independent monitors illustrate the spatial and psychological distance between them. The former housekeeper's body reacts with a trembling voice and tears to the memories elicited by the questions, after her experience of having to do housework for another family and raise their child in an unfamiliar country while her own child was growing up alone in the Philippines. In *Our Joyful Young Days*, the speakers are workers at a small factory. The questions they hear, unexpectedly, are about their memories of first love. Their surprise can be sensed in the physical responses when they first begin to speak. At first, they react with shy refusal: "I'm over 60 now! Why do you want me thinking about my first love?" But in addition to the smiles and sheepish laughter evoked by the blushing faces, they share stories that are distant and unfamiliar yet oddly close to us, combining nostalgia for their past infatuated selves with a sense of sadness and regret. Summoned back so suddenly and unexpectedly into their current lives of labor, the memories of first love pause those working lives and poke their heads up, while the artist transforms the stories into works of painting.

Having spent his life investigating the topic of recalling the past and lived

받고 지나간 시간을 떠올리는 대답자들이 등장한다. 때로 어떤 질문들은 우리에게 있던 깊숙한 기억을 휘저어 불러내는데, 그때 우리의 신체는 암기했던 답안을 상기하는 기계적 회상에서는 없는, 감정적 동요를 경험한다. 〈Q&A〉에서는 한 때 고용주이자 그 집의 재택 가정부로 한 집에서 생활했던 두 사람이 대화를 나눈다. 독립된 두 대의 모니터가 이들 사이의 공간적, 심리적 간극을 드러낸다. 자신의 아이는 필리핀에서 홀로 자라는 동안, 낯선 나라 가정의 가사를 돌보고 그 집의 아이를 양육해야 했던 여인의 신체는 질문이 불러낸 기억으로 인해 목소리가 떨리고 눈물을 흘리며 반응한다. 〈기쁜 우리 젊은 날〉의 대답자들은 크지 않은 공장에서 일하는 노동자들이다. 이들이 맞닥뜨린 질문은 뜬금없게도 첫사랑의 기억에 대한 것이다. 이 뜬금없음은 처음 말문을 열 때의 이들의 신체적 반응을 통해 감지된다. "지금 나이 육십 넘어 첫사랑 생각해서 뭘, 어쩌려는 거여!"라는 처음의 쑥스러운 거부 반응은, 상기된 얼굴에 떠오른 미소와 멋쩍은 웃음과 더불어, 한때 그런 사랑에 빠졌던 자신에 대한 그리움이, 일말의 서글픔과 회한과 결합된 멀고 낯설지만 기이하게 가까운, 이야기들로 이어진다. 현재의 노동하는 삶에, 갑작스럽고 뜬금없이 소환된 첫사랑에의 기억이, 노동하는 삶을 잠시 '중단'시키며 불쑥 고개를 내밀고, 작가는 이들의 이야기들을 그림으로 옮긴다.

지나간 것, 살았던 삶을 떠올리는 걸 평생의 화두로 삼았던 벤야민은 말년에 쓴 글에서 기억에 대해 이렇게 말한다.

> "기억(Gedächtnis)이라는 말은 기억이 과거를 탐색하는 도구가 아니라 과거가 펼쳐지는 무대라는 것을 오해의 여지 없이 밝혀준다. 땅이 죽은 도시들이 묻혀있는 매개체이듯 기억은 체험했던 것(Erlebten)의 매개체이다. 묻혀있는 자신의 과거에 다가가려는 사람은 땅을 파헤치는 사람처럼 행동해야 한다. 이것이 진정한 상기(Erinnerung)의 어조와 태도를 규정한다. 진정한 기억에서는 똑같은 내용을 반복해서 떠올리는 것을 기피해서는 안 된다. 흙을 뿌리듯이 기억의 내용을 뿌리고, 땅을 파듯이 그 내용을 파헤치는 것을 기피해서는 안 된다."[14]

과거는 지금은 사라진 죽은 도시들처럼 땅 속 깊은 곳에 묻혀있다. 땅 위에서 눈에 보이는 것만을 찾는 자는 결코 그를 찾을 수 없다. 진정한 상기를 위해서는 흙을 흩뿌리고, 땅을 파헤치는 신체적 움직임이 요구된다. 묻혀있는 기억을 발굴하려면 미술에도 그런 것이 필요할 것이다.

[14]
발터 벤야민, 『1900년경 베를린의 유년시절/베를린 연대기』, 윤미애 옮김(서울: 도서출판 길, 2007), 191. 번역 일부 수정.

묻혀있는 기억을 발굴하기: 미술과 기억

[14]
Walter Benjamin, *A Berlin Chronicle/Berlin Childhood around 1900*, trans. Yoon Mie (Seoul: Gil, 2007), 191.

experiences, Benjamin wrote the following about memory in one of his later works:

"The word Gedächtnis ['memory' in German] shows unambiguously that memory is not a tool for investigating the past, but a stage upon which the past unfolds. Just as the earth is a medium in which dead cities lie buried, memory is the medium for the experienced [Erlebten]. Those who wish to access the past buried within them must behave as those digging in the ground. This is what decides the tone and attitude of true remembering [Erinnerung]. In true remembering, we cannot shy away from recalling the same content over and over. We cannot neglect to scatter the content of memory like dust, and to delve into its content as we dig into the earth." [14]

Like a dead city that is no longer present, the past lies buried deep in the ground. It will never be found by those who look only for what can be seen above the surface. True remembering demands the physical movements of scattering dust and delving into the soil. Art too may need such things if it is to uncover buried memories.

비체험 세대의 다층적 기억 구성과 재현

배주연
서강대학교 트랜스내셔널인문학연구소

Multi-layered Memory Construction and Representation by Future Generations without Personal Experience

Bae Juyeon
Professor at Critical Global Studies Institute,
Sogang University

서강대학교 트랜스내셔널
인문학연구소 연구교수,
서울국제여성영화제 집행위원.
동시대 동아시아 영화를 비롯해
게임이나 시각예술에서 여성,
기억의 재현 양상 등 주제를
연구하고 있다.

A research professor at the
Sogang University Critical
Global Studies Institute
and member of the Seoul
International Women's Film
Festival executive committee,
Bae Juyeon researches
contemporary East Asian cinema,
representations of women in
games and the visual arts, and
the representational forms of
memory.

폭력의 기억을 어떻게 재현할 것인가?

20세기의 전쟁, 제노사이드, 폭력에 관한 기억을 어떻게 재현할 것인가는 현대미술의 중요한 화두 중의 하나였다. 그것은 재현 가능한가? 가능하다면 어떻게 가능한가? 폭력적 사건을 다시 재현함으로써 외상적 기억을 끄집어내는 것이 옳은 것인가? 상상력을 동원하여 사건을 형상화한다는 것의 비윤리성을 우리는 어떻게 견뎌야 할까? 이런 아포리아에 대해 아도르노는 아우슈비츠 이후 서정시를 쓰는 것의 야만성을 이야기했고, 모리스 블랑쇼는 상상조차 할 수 없는 끔찍한 인종말살의 행위(홀로코스트)를 문학이라는 상상적 글쓰기 대상으로 삼는 것 자체에 문제를 제기하며, 적극적인 재현의 거부와 침묵을 요청하였다. 반면 아감벤은 재현하지 않는 것은 이미지의 완전한 소거를 꿈꾸었던 나치의 절멸 시도에 동조하는 것이라 비판했고, 조르주 디디-위베르만은 『모든 것을 무릅쓴 이미지들』에서 수용소에서 건져낸 사진들이 전하는 긴박한 요청에 우리의 상상력을 가동해 적극적으로 응답할 것을 호소했다.[1] 아우슈비츠의 생존자였던 프리모 레비는 자신의 수용소 경험에 대해 단 한 점의 누락도 허용하지 않겠다는 듯 필사적으로 자신의 기억을 헤집어 글로 옮겼다.

이러한 재현의 곤경, 혹은 그 반대로 재현의 필연성은 공히 어떻게 재현할 것인가의 문제와 더불어 누가 재현할 수 있을 것인가, 즉 경험의 당사자와 비당사자 사이의 재현이라는 문제로 이어진다. 영화 「사울의 아들」의 감독이었던 라즐로 네메스가 "아우슈비츠에 대해 가장 잘 말할 수 있는 이들은 가스실에서 모두 죽었다"라고 말했을 때 그것은 기억의 당사자성을 명확하게 지시하는 말이었다. 사건을 경험조차 하지 않은 이들이 그것을 오롯이 재현할 수 있다는 것은 얼마나 어불성설인가? 그래서 네메스가 선택한 전략은 카메라의 시야각을 좁혀 수용소의 존더코만도(Sonderkommando)들에 집중하는 것이었다. 이런 점에서 디디-위베르만은 "암흑의 구멍"에서 벗어나기 위해 네메스가 선택한 (모든 것을 조망하는 시점이 아닌) 단거리의, 짧게 지속되는 불완전한 시점을 옹호했다.[2]

한편, 경험의 당사자성은 차학경, 루이즈 부르주아와 같은 1970년대 이후 페미니즘의 영향 속에서 자신의 외상적 기억을 끄집어냈던 페미니스트 여성 작가들에게도 중요한 의제가 되었다. 루이즈 부르주아는 "내가 관심을 갖는 많은 것들은 성차별이라는 개념 이전에, 내가 경험한 고통, 고독, 상처, 증오, 연민 등을 통해

[1]
자크 랑시에르, 『이미지의 운명』, 김상운 옮김(서울: 현실문화, 2014).

[2]
조르주 디디-위베르만, 『어둠에서 벗어나기』, 이나라 옮김(서울: 만일, 2015).

[1]
Jacques Rancière, *Le destin des images*, trans. Kim Sangun (Seoul: Hyunsil Munhwa, 2014).

[2]
Georges Didi-Huberman, *Sortir du noir*, trans. Yi Nara (Seoul: Wonny Story, 2015).

[3]
Bak Jeongmin, "Interview with Louise Bourgeois," *GQ Korea*, October 28, 2008.

How to Represent Memories of Violence?

One of the fundamental issues within contemporary art of the twentieth century was how to represent memories of war, genocide, and violence. Is it even possible to represent such forms of trauma? If so, how? Is it right to re-represent a violent event at the risk of arousing traumatic memories? How can we negotiate the seemingly impossible ethics of using imagination to delineate events?

Relating to this issue, Theodor Adorno said that writing poetry after Auschwitz was "barbaric," while Maurice Blanchot questioned the use of imagined literature to address the unimaginable horror of genocide (i.e., the Holocaust), which demands silence and a refusal of active representation. On the other hand, Giorgio Agamben condemned non-representation as ostensibly collaborating with the Nazi attempt to annihilate the image, which dreamed of complete erasure. Likewise, Holocaust survivor Primo Levi desperately scoured his memory for every possible detail he could recall about his experience in the camp, while Georges Didi-Huberman implored survivors to mobilize their imaginations and put out an urgent call for any existing photos of the concentration camps.[1]

Any discussion about the difficulty or, conversely, the necessity of representation inevitably leads to questions of how to represent and who is allowed to represent. In particular, what are the differences between representation by those who personally experienced a trauma and those who have only experienced it secondhand? Isn't it somewhat absurd to think that those who did not even experience an event could properly represent it? László Nemes, director of the Holocaust film *Son of Saul*, said that all those who could best speak about Auschwitz died in the gas chambers. As such, Nemes consciously narrowed the range of his film, choosing to focus solely on the "Sonderkommandos" (i.e., prisoners who were forced to work in the camps). In the same regard, rather than pursuing an all-encompassing viewpoint, Didi-Huberman opted for a limited and incomplete perspective in order to escape the "black hole."[2]

This issue has also been central for feminist artists, such as Theresa Hak Kyung Cha and Louise Bourgeois, who recovered their own memories of trauma through the influence of 1970s feminism. Bourgeois said, "Much of what interests me is the collection of emotions that I gained through pain, loneliness, wounds, hatred, compassion, etc., that I experienced firsthand before being introduced to the concept of sexism. I deal only with what I know and experience."[3] These questions of identity underscore the belief that those who have been deprived of their voice must personally speak about their own pain in order for healing to begin.

But these issues of memory and direct experience immediately invoke a difficult

얻은 감정의 집합이다. 나는 내가 알고 경험한 것만 다룬다"고 고백한다.[3] 그것은
언어를 박탈당한 이들이 자기 발화를 수행함으로써 정체성의 문제, 고통과 치유의
화두를 던지는 것이었다.

　　그러나 이런 당사자의 기억이라는 문제는 이내 곤경스러운 문제를 마주해야 했다.
사적으로 경험된 외상적 기억이 공동의 주의를 요청하는 것과는 달리, 광범위하게
이루어진 집단의 폭력을 상기할 때 그 기억의 당사자는 누구인가? 누가 그 기억의
소유권을 주장할 수 있는가? 그 기억을 간접적으로 혹은 느슨하게 공유하는 이들은
당사자인가 비당사자인가? '집합적 기억'(collective memory)의 개념을 제기한 모리스
알박스는 '집합적 기억'은 사적 기억과는 달리 집단 안에 분배된 개인의 기억이
전체의 부분적 이미지가 되는 것이라고 말한다.[4] 그렇다면 이미 우리가 마주하게
되는 기억은 직접 체험한 이들만의 기억일 순 없을 것이다. 무엇보다 기억의 당사자성
문제는 직접 체험자의 사후에 그 기억을 어떻게 계승할 것인가 하는 문제와도
연결된다.

　　또한, 오늘날 변화된 미디어 환경과 범람하는 미디어 이미지는 경험의 문제를
보다 복잡하게 만들었다. 일상적으로 전해지는 뉴스 방송은 전세계의 소식을 안방에서
지켜보도록 한다. 그리고 이렇게 미디어를 매개로 순환되는 어떤 사건들은 개인의
삶에 지대한 영향을 미친다. 어느 특정 세대에게 익숙한 만화영화나 유행가는 집단의
문화적 기억을 형성하기도 한다. 이에 대해 앨리슨 랜즈버그는 근대성이 공공의 문화
기억의 새로운 형식을 가능하게 할 뿐만 아니라 필연적으로 만든다고 주장하며 이러한
기억의 새로운 형식을 '보철의 기억'(prosthetic memory)이라고 명명한다. "내가
보철의 기억이라고 부르는 이러한 새로운 기억의 형식은 과거에 대한 역사적 서사와
개인 사이의 인터페이스에서, 극장이나 박물관과 같은 경험적 장소에서 출현한다.
이 접촉의 순간, 개인들은 자신을 보다 거대한 역사 속으로 봉합시킴으로써 경험이
생겨난다. [중략] 개인은 단순히 역사적 서사를 이해하는 것이 아니라 그 자신이 살지
않았던 과거 사건을 보다 개인적이고 깊게 느껴지는 기억으로 받아들이게 된다. 그
결과 보철의 기억은 개인의 주체성과 정치를 형성하는 능력을 갖는 것이다."[5] 오늘날
비체험된 사건도 체험이 될 수 있다는 점에서 체험/비체험, 당사자/비당사자의 문제는
훨씬 더 복잡한 양상을 띤다.

포스트메모리와 예술 작품

마리안느 허쉬는 직접 경험의 당사자들의 기억과 '이후 세대'(generations
after)들의 기억을 구분해 후자를 '포스트메모리'(post-memory)라고 불렀다.[6] 이들
'포스트메모리 세대'들은 자신들의 출생과 성장 과정에서 부모 세대들의 외상적
기억에 영향을 받고 자란 이들이다. 허쉬는 아트 슈피겔만의 그래픽 노블 『마우스』를
예로 들어 잠자리에서 부모 세대가 자녀 세대에게 들려주던 홀로코스트 경험을
통해 포스트메모리 세대의 기억 전수를 설명한다. 그는 포스트메모리가 "앞선
세대들이 기억하는 경험과 개인적, 집단적, 문화적 트라우마를 자신들의 어린 시절의

[3]
박정민, 「루이스 부르주아와의
인터뷰」, 『GQ』, 2008년 10월.

[4]
Maurice Halbwachs,
On Collective Memory, trans.
Lewis A. Coser (Chicago:
University of Chicago Press,
1992).

[5]
Alison Lansberg, *Prosthetic
Memory: The Transformation of
American Remembrance in the
Age of Mass Culture* (New York:
Columbia University Press,
2004).

[6]
Marianne Hirsch, *The
Generation of Postmemory:
Writing and Visual Culture
after the Holocaust* (New York:
Columbia University Press,
2012).

[4]
Maurice Halbwachs, *On Collective Memory*, trans. Lewis A. Coser (Chicago: University of Chicago Press, 1992).

[5]
Alison Landsberg, *Prosthetic Memory: The Transformation of American Remembrance in the Age of Mass Culture* (New York: Columbia University Press, 2004).

[6]
Marianne Hirsch, *The Generation of Postmemory: Writing and Visual Culture after the Holocaust* (New York: Columbia University Press, 2012).

[7]
Ibid, 5.

[8]
Giovanna Morra, "Contemporary Art Inside the Freud Museum: Working-Through Transit Documents, Postmemory, and the Holocaust," trans. Joo Ha Young, *Journal of History of Modern Art*, no. 26 (2009), 274–303.

problem. As opposed to individuals with memories of personal trauma that demand wider attention, who gets to claim ownership of memories of collective trauma perpetrated on a wide scale? Where do we draw the line between direct and indirect experience of such events? Maurice Halbwachs proposed the concept of collective memory, in which the memory of an individual within the group becomes a partial image of the whole.[4] But in such case, the memories that each individual faces are not based solely on personal experience. This issue becomes even more significant when thinking about how to preserve the memory of a traumatic event after all those who directly experienced the event have died.

The issue is even further complicated by the current environment of ubiquitous media and imagery. Each day, we are inundated with news reports from around the world, most of which pertain to events that have had a profound impact on individual lives. Moreover, the cultural memory of a group or generation also includes movies, cartoons, pop songs, etc. Alison Landsberg contends that, in the modern age, this new form of public cultural memory, which she termed "prosthetic memory," is not merely possible, but inevitable: "[P]rosthetic memory…emerges at the interface between a person and a historical narrative about the past, at an experiential site such as a movie theater or museum. In this moment of contact, an experience occurs through which the person sutures himself or herself into a larger history…[T]he person does not simply apprehend a historical narrative but takes on a more personal, deeply felt memory of a past event through which he or she did not live. The resulting prosthetic memory has the ability to shape that person's subjectivity and politics."[5] In a world where we are constantly invited to experience events that we did not actually experience, questions related to direct experience, indirect experience, and no experience have never been more complex.

Postmemory and Works of Art

Marianne Hirsch distinguishes between the firsthand memories of people who directly experienced an event and the "postmemory" of the "generation after," who grew up influenced by their parent's traumatic memories of the event.[6] For example, Hirsch uses Art Spiegelman's graphic novel *Maus* as an example of how parents' direct memories of the Holocaust were transmitted to the postmemory generation (i.e., their children) as bedtime stories. As Hirsch explains, postmemory "describes the relationship that the 'generation after' bears to the personal, collective, and cultural trauma of those who came before—to experiences they 'remember' only by means of the stories, images, and behaviors among which they grew up."[7] Hence, unlike those with direct experience of traumatic events, postmemory generations undergo belated trauma through mediated memories of those events.

Giovanna Morra invokes postmemory and belated trauma in discussing an exhibition at the Freud Museum by artists of the "generation after" who were exposed to memories of the Holocaust as children, or even before being born. Morra writes, "Freud's concepts can be extended to the infinite scope of psychoanalysis for transgenerational trauma recipients. As such, the work of postmemory is also always continuous and endless…In other words, the work of the postmemory in the production of these works is created by movement, memory, repetition, and continuous insight, which is always continuous and endless, belatedly persisting even after the event."[8]

이야기, 이미지, 그리고 행위들을 통해 견지하게 되는 '이후 세대'와의 관계"에 관여한다고 말한다.[7] 포스트메모리 세대의 기억은 직접 당사자들과는 달리 뒤늦게 경험되는 외상적 사건이다. 지오반나 모라는 자신의 출생 이전에, 혹은 유년기에 홀로코스트를 경험한 작가들이 프로이트 박물관에서 열었던 첫 전시회를 연구하며 포스트메모리와 이후 세대의 '뒤늦은 외상'의 경험을 논한다. "세대를 넘는 외상의 수혜자를 위한 정신분석학의 무한함으로 프로이트의 개념이 확장되는 것은 가능하다. 그로써, 포스트메모리의 작업은 또한 항상 계속되고 끝없는 것이다. 그리고 이것은 내가 말할 작품의 핵심이다. 즉, 이러한 작품 제작 안의 포스트메모리의 작업은 이동, 기억, 반복, 계속되는 통찰에 의해 만들어진 것이고, 이것은 항상 지속되고, 끝이 없고, 사건 이후까지, 뒤늦게 계속된다."[8] 여기에서 모라는 포스트메모리를 이후 세대들이 경험하는 트라우마적 기억, 즉 직접 체험 세대가 겪는 트라우마와 구별되면서도 뒤늦게 찾아와 그럼에도 여전히 '외상'으로 남는 기억들이라고 말한다. 즉, 비체험 세대의 기억은 이와 같은 외상(이라고 상정되어진 것)에 반응하며 그것을 확장하거나 저항하거나 교섭하며 만들어진다는 것이다. 이는 부모 세대의 해소되지 않은 멜랑콜리가 자녀 세대에게 미치는 외상적 기억이다. 이런 점에서 정연심은 '포스트메모리'를 '사후 기억'(post memory), '부재하는 기억'(absent memory), '때늦은 기억'(belated memory), '전승된 기억'(inherited memory) 등의 다양한 이름과 연결한다.[9]

반면, 이후 세대의 기억 작업을 외상적 기억에 의해 구성되고 작동하는 것이 아니라 현재에 과거를 개입시키는 적극적 정치 행위로 보는 이들도 있다. 예를 들면, 사무엘 오도너휴는 포스트메모리를 정신분석학의 외상적 기억과 연결시키는 것을 거부하고, 포스트메모리 작업은 액티비즘이지 이후 세대에 의해 감지된 사후 효과의 심리적 상흔의 결과가 아니라고 말한다.[10] 제프리 맥과이어 역시 아르헨티나의 경우 포스트 세대들의 기억 작업이 아르헨티나에서 일어난 집단적 희생에 대한 광범위한 이해를 바탕으로 이루어진다고 말하며, 가족 상실의 개인적 서사라는 가정(假定)에 주목하는 것이자 동시에 미디어로 인해 정치화되고 추동된 이미지로 자녀 세대들을 만들어낸 것에 대한 책임으로써 액티비즘의 형태를 취한다고 논한다.[11] 맥과이어가 주목하는 아르헨티나의 사례는 국가에 의해 자행된 부모 세대의 대규모 실종 사건 이후, 2세대가 성장하였을 때 이미 국가 주도의 이행기 정의가 진행 중인 상황이었다. 그래서 맥과이어는 2세대들에게 중요한 것은 실종자들의 존재 증명이 아니라 과거와 개인(이후 세대)이 맺는 관계의 의미를 모색하는 것이었고, 그로 인해 개인의 서사를 공적 장에 발화함으로써 국가 주도의 집단 기억의 서사에 개입하는 정치적 의미를 지닌다고 지적한다.

아르헨티나의 사례에서 포스트메모리 작업이 국가가 마련한 공적 기억의 장에 맞서 사적 관계의 중요성을 강조하는 것이었다면, 허쉬 역시 다른 맥락에서 가족 사진 등을 바탕으로 가족 내에서 일어나는 기억의 전수에 초점을 맞춘다. 이주의 경험을 바탕으로 한 데보라 윌리스의 사진 작업이나 아르헨티나의 유대인 공동체를 다룬

[7]
Ibid, 5.

[8]
지오반나 모라, 「프로이트 박물관 속의 동시대의 미술: 이동증명서, 포스트메모리, 그리고 홀로코스트를 통한 통찰」, 주하영 옮김, 『현대미술사연구』 제26집(2009), 274-303.

[9]
정연심, 「크리스티앙 볼탕스키의 '지연된 기억'(deffered memory)과 애도」, 『크리스티앙 볼탕스키: 4.4』 전시 도록(부산: 부산시립미술관, 2021).

[10]
Samuel O'Donoghue, "Postmemory as Trauma?: Some Theoretical Problems and Their Consequences for Contemporary Literary Criticism," Passés Futurs 3 (2018).

[11]
Geoffrey Maguire, The Politics of Postmemory: Violence and Victimhood in Contemporary Argentine Culture (London: Palgrave Macmillan, 2017).

[9]
Chung Yeon-shim, "Christian Boltanski's "Deferred Memory" and Remembrance" *Lee Ufan and His Friends III: Christian Boltanski 4.4* (Busan: Busan Museum of Art, 2021).

[10]
Samuel O'Donoghue, "Postmemory as Trauma?: Some Theoretical Problems and Their Consequences for Contemporary Literary Criticism," *Passés Futurs 3* (2018).

[11]
Geoffrey Maguire, *The Politics of Postmemory: Violence and Victimhood in Contemporary Argentine Culture* (London: Palgrave Macmillan, 2017).

[12]
Kang Kyoung-Lae, "The Recent Cinematic Depiction of Comfort Women and Its Cultural Significance in Korean Society: Examined through 'Post-Memory Generation' Discourse," *Journal of Humanities, Seoul National University*, vol. 75, no. 4 (2018), 229–262.

[13]
Dilara Çalı kan, "Queer Postmemory," *European Journal of Women's Studies*, vol. 26 no. 3 (2019), 261–273.

Here, Morra differentiates between memories of direct experience and postmemory, the traumatic memories belatedly experienced by later generations, which persist as trauma. Postmemory is created in response to supposed trauma when parents' traumatic memories of unresolved anguish are transmitted to their children. In the process, postmemory inevitably expands, resists, or negotiates with the original event, resulting in recurring trauma. In this respect, Chung Yeon-shim connects postmemory with related terms, such as "postmemoir," "absent memory," "belated memory," and "inherited memory."[9]

However, some have argued that works of postmemory produced by later generations are an autonomous political act pulling the past into the present, rather than something constructed and controlled by traumatic memories. For example, rejecting the psychoanalytic association between postmemory and traumatic memory, Samuel O'Donoghue asserts that postmemory works are examples of activism, rather than the results of psychological wounds inflicted on later generations.[10] Moreover, Geoffrey Maguire claims that the postmemory work of later generations related to the "Dirty War" in Argentina has been based on a broad understanding of the nation's collective sacrifice. Maguire agrees that such work takes the form of activism, simultaneously acknowledging personal narratives of family loss while taking responsibility for the later generations whose memories are being shaped by politicized media images.[11] Significantly, in Argentina, the state's attempt to redefine the traumatic events was already underway when the children of "disappeared" parents were growing up. In this context, Maguire stresses that the priority for this postmemory work was not to prove the existence of the missing, but rather to allow individual members of the "generation after" to find meaning in their relationship between the past. Sharing one's individual narrative with the public thus becomes a political act helping to contravene the state's attempt to shape the collective memory of the nation.

Like Maguire, Hirsch has also examined how postmemory work in Argentina has served to emphasize the importance of private relationships against the public memory shaped by the state. However, Hirsch focused on family photos, such as Mirta Kupferminc's graphic works of the Jewish community in Argentina and Deborah Willis's photos of migration experiences. Expanding memory beyond private relationships, Hirsch divides postmemory into familial postmemory, or memories passed down from parents to children, and affiliative memory, in which members of the same generation collectively consider and elaborate upon the memories that they have been given. Regarding this communal expansion of postmemory, Kang Kyoung-Lae wrote, "The perspective of the post-memory generation highlights the ethical obligation of future generations (who have shared the intimate memories of their ancestors' suffering) to others who remain vacant in their identities."[12] While memories passed down within a family take the form of belated trauma, the memories shared within later generations become an ethical response to others. In response to Hirsch's "familial postmemory," which seems to assume a heteronormative family, Dilara Çalı kan has proposed "queer postmemory."[13]

Since the dissemination of memories takes place in myriad ways, postmemory cannot be understood simply as the process of transmission between parents and children. For example, Alison Landsberg has noted how memory is becoming increasingly dependent on media as communities and families are dissolved. In

마리타 쿠퍼밍크의 그래픽 작품이 대표적인 예이다. 그러나 허쉬는 포스트메모리를 가족적 포스트메모리(familial post-memory)와 제휴적 포스트메모리(affiliative memory)로 구분하여 사적 관계를 넘어선 기억의 확장 가능성을 열어둔다. 즉 부모와 자식 사이의 간-세대적 기억의 전승이 한 축에 있다면, 다른 한 축에서는 아이에게 전수된 기억이 확장되는 세대 내적 동일시의 작업이 있다는 것이다. 강경래는 이러한 포스트메모리의 공동체적 확장에 대해 "포스트-기억 세대의 시각은 선조들이 겪은 고초에 대한 내밀한 기억들을 공유한 후세대들이 자신들의 정체성에 있어 빈자리로 남아 있는 타자에 대해 갖는 윤리적 의무라는 측면을 부각시킨다"고 지적한다.[12] 즉, 가족 내에서 일어나는 이후 세대들의 기억이 뒤늦은 외상이라는 형태라면, 이후 세대들의 공동의 기억이라는 문제는 타자에 대한 윤리적 반응이라는 것이다. 한편, 허쉬의 가족적 포스트메모리 역시 자명한 것은 아닌데, 그것이 상정하고 있는 가족이 이성애 규범적 가족이라는 점에서 딜라라 찰리스칸은 '퀴어 포스트메모리'(queer postmemory)를 제기한 바 있다.[13]

이처럼 포스트메모리는 단순히 부모 세대와 자식 세대 간의 전수 과정으로만 이해할 수는 없다. 또한 랜즈버그가 보철의 기억을 논하며 오늘날 공동체나 가족이 해체되어가면 갈수록 기억은 점점 더 미디어에 의존할 수밖에 없다고 이야기한 것처럼, 기억의 전수와 전파는 더욱 다양하게 이루어지고 있다. 따라서, 최근의 포스트메모리 세대의 작업들은 가족, 혹은 이른바 '정상 가족'의 프레임을 넘어 기억의 계승 과정의 확장을 꾀하고 있다. 물론 에바 호프만이 "2세대와 포스트 세대의 기억을 구분하여야 한다"[14]고 주장한 것처럼 가족 내의 기억의 전수와 세대 내 기억의 전달은 그 형성과 전개에서 동일한 과정을 거치는 것은 아니다. 그렇다면, 직접적 체험의 당사자도 아닐뿐더러 부모의 트라우마와 함께 성장하면서 가정 안에서 뒤늦은 외상적 체험을 겪은 2세대도 아닌 이들은 어떻게 외상적 경험에 동일시하고 친밀성의 관계(제휴적 포스트메모리)를 획득할 수 있는가?

이에 대해 허쉬는 이후 세대의 기억 형성에 있어 포스트메모리적 정동을 이야기한 바 있다. 그는 롤랑 바르트의 사진의 매혹에 관한 두 가지 개념, 스투디움과 푼크툼을 가지고 와서 과거의 기억과 대면한 이들에게 말을 걸어 찌르는 듯한 푼크툼의 정동 획득을 이야기한다. 그것은 명확하게 다가갈 수 있는 실체로서 존재하는 기억이 아니라 어느 순간 다가와 해소되지 못하고 지속되는 강도로서의 정동이다.

"포스트메모리는 문화적 혹은 집단적 트라우마를 목격한 이들의 다음 세대가 그전 세대의 경험과 맺게 되는 관계를 묘사한다. 그런데 그 경험은 오직 자라면서 알게 된 이야기나 이미지 그리고 행위라는 수단을 통해서만 그들이 '기억하는' 경험이다. 하지만 이러한 경험은 자신들의 방식으로 기억을 구성하는 것과도 같이 강력하고 감응적으로 다음 세대에게 전달된다. 포스트메모리가 과거와 연결되는 것은 따라서 회상에 의해서가 아니라 오히려 상상적 투사, 반영, 그리고 창조에 의해 매개된다."[15]

여기에서 눈여겨볼 것은 바로 포스트메모리가 매개된 기억이라는 점이다. 제임스 E. 영 역시 이후 세대들의 기억은 역사의 사후적 이미지들(after-images)에 의해

[12]
강경래, 「'위안부' 피해자 영상의 "포스트-기억 세대" 양식으로의 변화와 사회문화적 함의 읽기」, 『인문논총』 75권, 4호(2018), 229-262.

[13]
Dilara Çalı kan, "Queer Postmemory," European Journal of Women's Studies, vol. 26, no. 3 (2019), 261-273.

[14]
Eva Hoffman, After Such Knowledge: Memory, History, and the Legacy of the Holocaust (New York: PublicAffairs, 2004).

[15]
Hirsch, The Generation of Postmemory: Writing and Visual Culture after the Holocaust.

[14]
Eva Hoffman, *After Such Knowledge: Memory, History, and the Legacy of the Holocaust* (New York: PublicAffairs, 2004).

[15]
Hirsch, *The Generation of Postmemory: Writing and Visual Culture after the Holocaust.*

[16]
James E. Young, *At Memory's Edge: After-images of the Holocaust in Contemporary Art and Architecture* (London: Yale University Press, 2000).

[17]
Lucie Angheben, "De l'indicible du témoignage au non-dicible de la fiction: vers une nouvelle représentation de Gwangju dans la littérature coréenne? - Autour de la nouvelle «Alors que faut-il chanter?» de Park Sol-moe et de sa traduction en français," *Comparative Korean Studies,* vol.26, no.1 (2018), 173–211.

accordance, many recent postmemory works have moved beyond the frame of the family, or at least the so-called "typical" family. Recalling Eva Hoffman's distinction between the memory of the second generation and the post-generation, there are major differences in the ways that memories are transmitted within a family and within an entire generation.[14] Under these conditions, how can later generations, who neither directly experienced a traumatic event nor even belatedly experienced the event through the memories of their parents, come to identify with the event and acquire an affiliative postmemory?

In contemplating this issue, Hirsch borrows the concepts of the "studium" (i.e., initial attraction) and "punctum" (i.e., deeper meaning or interest) taken from Roland Barthes's study of photography. In the context of postmemory, Hirsch posits that later generations are "pricked" with punctum by talking to those who directly experienced events of the past. Rather than entities that can easily approached, such memories are an affect or intensity that approaches people and persists without being resolution. As Hirsch describes, "These experiences were transmitted to them so deeply and affectively as to seem to constitute memories in their own right. As I see it, the connection to the past that I define as postmemory is mediated not by recall but by imaginative investment, projection, and creation."[15] As illustrated by James E. Young's analysis of after-images of history, postmemory is an intermediated experience for later generations, or the afterlife of memory.[16]

The inherent complexity of these intermediary memories, which are transmitted both across generations and within generations, is exemplified by the work of Christian Boltanski (b. 1944), who may be seen as a postmemory artist. As a child, Boltanski encountered death and trauma through the memories of his Jewish father, who had escaped the Holocaust by hiding under a hardwood floor. These memories became a primary motif in Boltanski's artworks, but only after being reprocessed and filtered through various media of the twentieth century. For example, rather than trying to evoke trauma by directly representing his father's experience, Boltanski instead created installations from photos of other people that he had collected. His choice of media also reflects the lack of photos from his own childhood. The "absence" behind the "presence" of his works is connected to his parents' memories of the Holocaust. But while his works such as *Monument* and *Reserve: The Festival of Purim* take the form of a memorial altar with enlarged black-and-white photos, the people in the photos are not actually victims of the Holocaust, but arbitrary deceased people from photos that he collected. Boltanski's installation *The Memory of Childhood* also featured photos of anonymous people with no relation to the artist, while *Altar of the Detective* contained photos of performers, criminals, and victims that the artist cut out from crime magazines, blending their identities. Such works not only evoke cultural memories formed through mass media, but also create new ones by rearranging the photos and erasing their original context. As opposed to simply recording statistics or testimonies, these postmemory works rely upon a unique combination of facts and imagination. Lucie Angheben, who has studied historical literature by authors of subsequent generations who did not live through the depicted period, believes that it is impossible to be a witness to a history that one has not personally experienced. In such literature, she writes, "We witness a transition from witnesses to heirs, from one generation to another, and hence from testimony literature to fiction."[17] Rather than testimony or interrogation about what happened, the postmemory works of Christian Boltanski and contemporaneous artists

재현되는 매개된 경험, 기억의 사후적 삶(afterlife of memory)이라고 말한 바 있다.[16]

　　포스트메모리 세대인 크리스티앙 볼탕스키의 작업은 이러한 매개된, 세대 내, 세대 간 기억의 전수를 복합적으로 보여준다. 그는 1944년생으로 홀로코스트를 피해 마룻바닥에 숨어 지내야했던 유대인 아버지와 함께 어린 시절을 보냈다. 그리고 그는 자신의 유년시절 마주해야 했던 죽음의 기억을 작품의 제재로 삼았다. 그러나, 그의 작업은 트라우마를 환기시키거나 자신의 기억을 직접적으로 재현하기보다 미디어가 매개하는 20세기 죽음의 이미지를 다시금 재가공하고 작동시키는 방식으로 이루어졌다. 그는 주로 타인들의 사진을 수집하고, 수집된 사진들로 설치물을 만들었다. 그의 이러한 작업은 그 자신의 어린 시절 사진의 부재와도 맞닿아 있다. 즉, 그의 작업의 '현전' 이면의 '부재'가 부모 세대의 홀로코스트의 기억과 연결된다. 다른 한편, ‹기념비›, ‹저장소: 퓨림 축제›와 같이 흑백의 사진을 확대해 제단 형식으로 만든 작품들은 마치 홀로코스트 희생자들을 연상시키지만, 이는 실제 희생자들이 아닌 그가 수집한 사진들에서 가공된 죽음의 이미지다. 마찬가지로 ‹어린 시절의 기억›은 작가 자신과는 관련 없는 익명의 사람들의 사진들을 패널에 부착한 설치물이며, ‹탐정의 제단›은 범죄물 잡지에서 그가 오려낸 배우, 범죄자, 희생자의 사진을 재단 형식으로 구상해 이들에게 부여되었던 정체성을 혼합시켜버린다. 그의 이러한 작업은 사진에 원래 부여되었던 맥락을 소거하고, 그 사진들을 다른 맥락 속에 재배치함으로써 대중 매체가 형성한 문화적 기억을 환기할 뿐만 아니라 새로운 기억을 창조하기도 한다. 이는 사실을 기록하고 증언하는 것과는 달리 사실의 새로운 조합과 상상을 요청하는 작업이다. 비체험 세대의 문학을 연구한 뤼시 앙게벤은 경험하지 않은 역사에 대해 증인이 되는 것은 불가능하다고 말하며, "우리는 증인에서 상속자로, 한 세대에서 다른 세대로의 이행, 따라서 증언문학에서 픽션으로의 이행을 목격하게 된다"고 지적한다.[17] 이와 같이 볼탕스키나 동시대 작가들의 포스트메모리 작업은 일어난 일의 증언과 심문을 위한 작업이 아닌, 우리의 상상력을 어떻게 과거의 사건과 조우시킬 것인가의 문제를 제기한다.

아카이브, 기록, 애도

최근 동시대 한국 작가들에게서도 포스트메모리 작업은 어렵지 않게 목격된다. 제인 진 카이젠의 ‹이별의 공동체›, 정은영의 ‹여성국극 프로젝트›를 비롯해 송상희, 임흥순, 최원준, 김오안 등 많은 작가들이 과거의 기억과 지금이 만나는 관계를 탐색하고 있다. 혹은 조해준 작가처럼 아버지와의 협업을 통해 한국 근대사의 전쟁과 폭력을 경험한 부모 세대의 기억과 조우를 모색하기도 한다.

　　근래에 다양하게 이루어지고 있는 포스트메모리 세대들의 작업에는 생존자들의 죽음으로 인한 증언의 부재, 미디어가 생산하는 과거의 이미지와 작가의 관계, 그리고 탈진실의 시대라는 맥락이 자리한다. 앞서 지적한 것처럼 허쉬는 포스트메모리는 더 이상 회상에 의해 과거와 연결되는 것이 아니라 상상적 투사, 반영, 그리고 창조에 의해 매개된다고 이야기했는데, 이럴 때 공백으로 남게 되는 사실에 대한 앎의 욕망 역시

[16]
James E. Young, *At Memory's Edge: After-images of the Holocaust in Contemporary Art and Architecture* (London: Yale University Press, 2000).

[17]
뤼시 앙게벤, 「증언의 형언불가능성에서 픽션의 말할 수 없음으로: 광주의 새로운 재현을 지향하는 한국문학? - 박솔뫼의 그럼 무얼 부르지와 프랑스어 번역」, 『비교한국학』, 26권, 1호(2018), 173-211.

[18]
Hal Foster, "An Archival Impulse," *October*, vol. 110 (2004), 3–22.

[19]
Hal Foster et al., *Art Since 1900*, trans. Bae suhee et al. (Seoul: Semicolon, 2016), 786.

instead ask how we can use our imagination to confront past events.

Archives, Documentation, and Mourning

Postmemory works are relatively easy to find in contemporary Korean art. Along with Jane Jin Kaisen's *Community of Parting* and Siren Eun Young Jung's *Yeoseong Gukgeuk* project, artists such as Song Sanghee, Im Heung-soon, Choi Won Jun, and Kim Oan are actively exploring the relationship between our memories of the past and our lives in the present. In addition, Cho Haejun, collaborating with his father, explores the previous generation's firsthand memories of the Korean War and other episodes of violence in contemporary Korean history. Given the increasing difficulty of finding testimony about these events, due to the ongoing deaths of those with firsthand experience, these postmemory artworks have become more diverse in recent years, examining the relationship between the artist and media images of the past within the era of post-truth. As Hirsch explained, postmemory is no longer connected to the past by personal recollection, but through imaginary projection, reflection, and creation.
Even so, the recovery of facts that have been lost or hidden remains crucial to these works. This desire for facts strongly influences which images, which information, and which news are considered to be true for the current generation, who are inundated with images, information, and news, much of which is fake. As media continues to expand and diversify, the flow of information will become even more profuse, meaning that firsthand memories will be less likely to be shared. Indeed, some of the postmemory works in this exhibition aim to document and mourn the death of witnesses.

As observed by Hal Foster, the death and disappearance of people with firsthand memories can sometimes stimulate the "archival impulse" to gather records and testimonies.[18] But in contemporary art, archives transcend the mere collecting and listing of facts. According to Foster, the contemporary archival impulse "is manifest in a will to make historical information, often lost, marginal, or suppressed, physical and spatial, indeed interactive, usually through found images, objects, and texts arranged in installations."[19] In *Auditorium (Template A–Z)* by Mioon, in which memories are symbolically expressed in the form of theater, five bookshelves are arranged in a semicircle, containing objects that are viewed as shadow images. These shadow images of familiar objects with some personal connection—such as a chair that once belonged to someone, a tombstone with a cross, and barbed wire (recalling the DMZ)—weave private and public memories together, recalling them within a surreal and dreamlike space. In summoning these ghosts of the uncanny past, the work suggests the similarity between dream and memory.

Song Joowon, who makes site-specific performance videos, presents *Pimple.Blister.Wart.Mole.* filmed at the former Armed Forces' Gwangju Hospital, a location associated with the Gwangju Uprising of 1980. The title of the work refers to various skin blemishes that can be physically or chemically removed from the body, yet still leave a scar. Similarly, this hospital (before recently being re-opened for the Gwangju Biennale) spent many years in ruins as an urban blemish, haunting the people of Gwangju with grievous memories from long ago. As such, the building itself is a massive archive. The artist's performance at the former hospital served as a type of ritual, infusing the desolate space with new meaning. Summoning the dead to rise from the debris, Song's performance frees the ghosts of the past, allowing them to once again

두드러지게 등장한다. 이런 사실에 대한 강박은 무수한 이미지와 가짜 뉴스, 정보들이 넘치는 세계를 살아가는 지금의 세대에게 어떤 이미지가, 어떤 정보가, 또 어떤 뉴스가 진실인가에 대한 질문과 연결된다. 미디어 플랫폼이 다양화될수록 이런 정보들은 더더욱 넘쳐나게 될 것이고, 그 날을 경험한 이들의 기억을 '말할 수 있는 입'은 점점 줄어들 것이다. 다른 한편에선 이러한 죽음에 맞서 생존자의 부재를 애도하고, 기록하고, 기억하는 자로서 자신을 자리매김하는 작가들의 작품이 있다. 아래에는 이번 전시에서 소개되는 비체험 세대의 포스트메모리 작업 몇 편을 살펴보고자 한다.

먼저, 증언할 수 있는 이들의 사라짐은 한편에선 필사적 기록과 증언의 필요성, 즉 아카이브 충동을 부추긴다.[18] 그러나 현대 미술에서 아카이브는 단순히 사실의 나열과 기록, 수집만을 의미하진 않는다. 할 포스터는 "보통 설치 안에 배열돼 있는 발견된 이미지, 오브제, 텍스트를 통해, 대개 망각되거나 주변적인 혹은 억압된 역사적 정보를 물리적이고 공간적인, 정말로 인터랙티브한 것으로 만들려는 의지"를 동시대의 아카이브 충동 속에서 발견한다.[19] 기억의 상징들을 극장 형식으로 표상한 뮌의 〈오디토리움(Template A-Z)〉은 다섯 개의 책장을 반원형의 구조로 배치하고, 책장 선반 위에 놓인 오브제들을 그림자 이미지로 관람하도록 한 작품이다. 한때 누군가에게 귀속되었을 의자, 십자가가 달린 묘비, 교각, 휴전선을 연상시키는 철조망과 같은 오브제들의 그림자 이미지는 사적 기억과 공적 기억의 장소들을 한 곳으로 엮어내고, 이를 다시 몽환적이고 초현실적인 공간으로 옮겨 놓는다. 그것은 기억의 회상과 꿈 작업의 유사성을 환기시키는 한편, 언캐니(uncanny)한 과거의 유령들을 소환한다.

장소 특정적 퍼포먼스 영상 작업을 하는 송주원의 〈뾰루지.물집.사마귀.점〉은 5·18 광주민중항쟁 당시의 현장 중 하나였던 국군광주병원에서 촬영되었다. 작품의 제목 속 뾰루지, 물집, 사마귀, 점은 신체 표면에 드러난 이상 신호들이다. 물리적, 화학적으로 제거할 수 있지만, 그것은 사라진 이후에도 언제든 표면 위에 제 흔적을 남길 수 있는 잠재적 존재로 남아 있는 것들이다. 최근에야 광주 비엔날레를 위해 오픈된 국군광주병원은 폐허의 모습으로 남아 40여 년 전의 상처와 죽음의 기억을 비통하게 불러낸다. 옛 국군광주병원에서 이루어지는 송주원의 퍼포먼스 작업은 일종의 제의이자, 다른 한편 죽어버린 공간에 새로운 의미들을 부여하는 작업이기도 하다. 오랫동안 방치된 채 폐허가 되어버린 국군병원은 그 자체로 거대한 아카이브다. 송주원의 퍼포먼스 작업은 그 잔해 위에 죽은 자를 불러내고 배회하는 유령들을 마주 세워 다시 움직임을 부여한다. 이러한 작업은 최근 동일한 장소에서 작업된 장민승의 작업 〈둥글고, 둥글게〉와 비교해볼 수 있다. 파운드 푸티지와 직접 촬영한 영상을 혼합해 만든 〈둥글고, 둥글게〉는 88서울올림픽의 기억에서부터 시작해 1980년 국군광주병원으로 시간을 거슬러 올라간다. 그리고 그곳에서 텅 빈 부재를 응시한다. 동일한 장소에서 유사한 카메라 워크로 촬영된 송주원의 작업 역시 죽음의 이미지를 상기시키지만, 그것은 부재한 것을 불러일으키고, 결여된 것을 채우는 몸짓으로 이루어진다는 점에서 흥미로운 대구를 이룬다.

[18]
Hal Foster, "An Archival Impulse," *October*, vol. 110 (2004), 3-22.

[19]
할 포스터 외, 『1900년 이후의 미술사』, 배수희 외 옮김(서울: 세미콜론, 2016), 786.

[20]
Tessa Morris-Suzuki, *Follow The Past Within Us: Media, Memory, History*, trans. Kim Gyeongwon (Seoul: Humanist, 2006).

move and face one another. The work can be compared to *Round and Around* by Jang Minseung, another recent performance at the same location. Combining found footage and video taken by the artist, *Round and Around* starts from memories of the 1988 Seoul Olympics before moving back to the hospital in 1980. Once there, the artist gazes into an empty void. Shot at the same site with similar styles, both works conjure the image of death, but also attempt to recover what is missing.

Park Hyesoo's *Our Joyful Young Days* is a split-screen video, showing workers of different ages and genders talking about their first love on one side while the artist paints portraits on the other side. While some of the people being interviewed cannot help but smile as they fondly recall their first love, others show regret for an unfulfilled love, or claim that thinking about their first love is an indulgence within their busy daily life. Meanwhile, on the other side of the screen, the faces in the artist's portraits are images in gestation, not yet fully formed. The close-up shots make it impossible to discern the faces as a whole, revealing only the artist's painting process. This work brings the forgotten daily lives of workers onto the screen, transforming their most private and intimate memories into a collective cultural memory. As such, it restores the memory of "everyday time," as opposed to "work time." At the same time, Ham Mina is constantly present as the one who records, imagines, and represents this memory. But if there is any correlation between the interviewees and the Ham Mina's portraits, it is never revealed. Instead, the work draws our attention to the act of painting, rather than the painting itself. The artist's role is to listen to other people's memories, and to imagine, mediate, and represent the characters in the story, becoming a bearer of memories.

From "Memories After" to Future Memories

Tessa Morris-Suzuki has asserted that Japan's postwar generations need to be more involved in atonement, as they cannot be absolved from the violent actions of previous generations.[20] Indeed, even those who did not personally experience a war cannot escape its lingering effects. Past violence that we did not personally experience is still woven into the present. In this sense, any efforts made by the "generation after" to face the memories of the past is not only an ethical response to others, but also an attempt to reflect on their own present life. Moreover, those who consume images of the past through today's media are not mere spectators, but participants in the representation of images. Beyond merely bringing the vanishing memories of previous generations into the present, postmemory work actively engages with the memories of the past that have already arrived in the present. For subsequent generations with only secondhad experience, representation can only occur through imagination and projection. But rather than trying to imagine what happened in a past that they did not experience, they must imagine a future in which they are directly involved.

박혜수의 〈기쁜 우리 젊은 날〉은 두 개의 분할화면으로 구성된 영상으로 이루어져
있다. 오른쪽에는 카메라 앞에 앉은 노동자들이 첫사랑에 관해 인터뷰를 하고 있다.
인터뷰를 하는 사람들은 나이도, 성별도, 첫사랑에 대한 기억도 상이하다. 누군가는
첫사랑과의 즐거웠던 기억을 떠올리며 연신 웃음을 짓는가 하면, 누군가는 못다
이룬 사랑에 대한 안타까움을 드러낸다. 또 누군가는 바쁜 일상 속에 첫사랑의
추억을 곱씹는 것은 사치라고 말하기도 한다. 인터뷰가 이어지는 동안 왼쪽 화면에선
인물화를 그리는 작가가 등장한다. 작가의 인물화 속 얼굴들은 정확한 형태를 갖추기
전의 이미지들로 클로즈업된 화면 속에서 전체의 윤곽을 드러내지 않는다. 오직
그림을 그리는 행위만이 뚜렷하게 보일 뿐이다. 이와 같은 박혜수의 작업은 한편에선
노동자들의 잊혀진 일상을 스크린 위로 불러와 지극히 사적이고 내밀한 기억이었던
것을 집단의 문화적 기억으로 만든다. 그것은 '노동의 시간'과 대비되는 '일상의
시간'에 대한 기억을 복원하는 작업이다. 다른 화면에서 함미나 작가는 이 기억을
기록하고 상상하여 재현하는 자로서 등장한다. 함미나 작가의 작업이 왼쪽 화면 속
인터뷰이들의 기억과 직접적인 상관관계를 가지는지는 알 수 없다. 그러나 여기에서
주목할 것은 함미나 작가가 그린 그림이 아닌 그리는 행위 자체에 화면의 초점이
맞춰져 있다는 점이다. 여기에서 작가는 타인의 기억을 경청하는 자(인터뷰어)이자,
이야기 속 인물들을 상상하고 매개하여 재현하는 자, 그리하여 기억의 전수자가 된다.

이후 기억에서 미래의 기억으로

테사 모리스 스즈키는 일본의 전후 세대 역시 이전 세대의 전쟁 책임에서 자유로울
수 없다고 말하며 '연루의 감각'을 가질 것을 제안한다.[20] 전쟁을 경험하지 않은
이도, 전쟁의 결과로 야기된 전후의 삶에서 자유로울 수 없기 때문이다. 체험되지
않은 과거의 폭력은 현재에 기입된다. 이런 의미에서 비체험 세대가 과거의 기억을
마주하는 것은 타인에 대한 윤리적 응답일 뿐만 아니라 현재의 삶에 대한 성찰적
태도이기도 하다. 더욱이 오늘날 미디어를 통해 전달되는 과거의 이미지를 소비하는
이들 역시 단순한 관람자가 아니라 이미지의 재현에 연루된 자들이다. 그러므로
포스트메모리는 사라져가는 이전 세대의 기억을 현재화하는 작업이 아니라 이미
현재에 당도한 과거의 기억과 마주하는 작업이다. 비체험 세대의 재현에 상상과
투사가 필요한 이유는 여기에 있다. 과거의 일어난 일에 대해 상상하는 것이 아닌
연루된 자로서 미래를 상상하기.

[20]
테사 모리스·스즈키, 『우리
안의 과거: 미디어, 메모리,
히스토리』, 김경원 옮김(서울:
휴머니스트, 2006).

비체험 세대의 다층적 기억 구성과 재현

기념하다,
함께-기억하다

최유미

연구자, 수유너머 104

Commemorate
and Com-memorate

Choi Yumi

Researcher, Suyunomo 104

한국과학기술원 화학과에서 이론 물리화학으로 박사학위를 받았고, 20년간 IT회사에 근무했다. 지금은 수유너머104에서 동서양의 철학을 횡단하면서 인문학을 공부하고 가르치는 삶을 살고 있다. 그 공부의 중심에 도나 해러웨이의 사상과 과학기술학, 그리고 비인간과 인간의 '함께 살기'에 대한 고민이 있다. 지은 책으로 『해러웨이, 공-산의 사유』, 『감응의 유물론과 예술』(공저) 등이 있으며 번역서로 『트러블과 함께 하기』, 『원자폭탄』(공동 번역)이 있다.

After earning a doctoral degree in theoretical physical chemistry from the KAIST chemistry department, Choi Yumi worked for 20 years in information technology. Today, she spends her time studying and teaching the humanities, working in between the fields of Eastern and Western philosophy at Suyunomo 104. Central to her studies are questions about the ideas of Donna Haraway, the academic exploration of science and technology, and the coexistence of human with non-human beings. She has written the book *Donna Haraway: Thinking of Sympoiesis* and co-authored the book *Materialism and Art in Affect*. She has also translated the book *Staying with the Trouble* and co-translated the book *Bomb*.

'그때, 그곳'[1]

지나간 시간은 되돌릴 수 없다. 하지만 누구도 '그때, 그곳'이 없다고는 말하지 못한다. '그때, 그곳'은 우리의 기억 속에서 의식적으로든 무의식적으로든 반복해서 불려 나오기 때문이다. 그래서 '그때, 그곳'은 하나의 시간과 공간을 점유하는 좌표계의 점이 아니라 반복적으로 되돌아오는 운동 속에 있다. 우리는 의식적인 방식으로 불려 나오는 '그때, 그곳'을 통상 역사라고 부른다. 『반시대적 고찰』에서 니체는 역사를 "기념비적", "골동품적", "비판적"인 것으로 분류한다.[2] 기념비적 역사는 과거의 찬란했던 '그때, 그곳'을 다시 반복시키기 위해 불려 나오고 골동품적 역사는 조상들의 귀중한 유산에 존경을 표하고 보존하기 위해 불려 나오고, 비판적 역사는 고통받고 원한에 사무친 과거를 해방하기 위해 불려 나온다. 이미 지나가 버린 '그때, 그곳'을 이렇게 불러내는 것은 삶을 위해 과거를 사용하기 위해서다.

하지만 과거를 삶에 봉사하게 하는 것은 쉬운 일이 아니다. 제때 기억하고 제때 잊어버리지 않으면 역사를 지나치게 진지하게 생각하는 질병이 바로 덮치기 때문이다. 니체가 경고했듯이 "역사의 과잉은 살아있는 것에 해를 끼친다."[3] 위대한 영웅의 역사든 지키고 보존해야 할 조상의 고귀한 유산이든 다시는 반복해선 안 될 비판의 역사이든 그것은 인간이 스스로를 조형하기 위해 필요한 것이지만 그것을 위해서는 상당한 정도의 능력이 필요하다.

> 과거의 것이 현재의 것의 무덤을 파지 않으려면, 과거의 것이 잊혀야 할 한도와 한계를 결정하기 위해서는 우리는 한 인간, 한 민족과 한 문화의 조형력이 얼마나 큰지를 정확하게 알아야 한다. 조형력이란 스스로 고유한 방식으로 성장하고, 과거의 것과 낯선 것을 변형시켜 자기 것으로 만들며, 상처를 치유하고 상실한 것을 대체하고 부서진 형식을 스스로 복제할 수 있는 힘을 말한다.[4]

건강한 삶을 무엇보다 중시한 니체는 기억할 수 없으면 행복하게 살아갈 수 있지만 망각 능력이 없으면 삶이 불가능하다고 역설한다. "비역사적인 상태에서 먼저 갈망하고 추구하지 않고는 어떤 예술가도 자신의 그림을, 어떤 장군도 승리를, 어떤 민족도 자유를 얻을 수 없다."[5] 역사를 구성하는 것은 인간의 능력이지만 자기가 만든 것을 부수는 능력이 없으면 삶을 갉아먹게 된다. 니체가 보기에 동물은 "거의

[1]
'그때, 그곳'과 '지금, 여기'는 전시 《나너의 기억》의 섹션명이기에 따옴표로 표시한다.

[2]
프리드리히 니체, 「반시대적 고찰」, 『비극의 탄생 반시대적 고찰』, 이진우 옮김(서울: 책세상, 2005), 301.

[3]
같은 책, 301.

[4]
같은 책, 293.

[5]
같은 책, 296.

기념하다, 함께-기억하다

[1]
"That Time, That Place" and
"Here and Now" are the titles
of the two sections of the
exhibition *My Your Memory*,
and are thus placed in quotation
marks.

[2]
Friedrich Nietzsche, "Thoughts
Out of Season" in *The Birth
of Tragedy/Thoughts Out of
Season*, trans. Lee Jin Woo
(Seoul: Chaeksesang, 2005),
301.

[3]
Ibid., 301.

[4]
Ibid., 293.

[5]
Ibid., 296.

"That Time, That Place" [1]

We can never return to the past, but neither can we say that the past does not exist, because "that time, that place" are constantly being summoned in our memory, either consciously or unconsciously. Thus, "that time, that place" are not a point in a system of coordinates, occupying a single moment or position in spacetime, but rather a motion of continuous repetition and return. When we consciously summon "that time, that place" it is called history. In *Untimely Meditations*, Friedrich Nietzsche identifies three approaches to history: the monumental, the antiquarian, and the critical.[2] Monumental history consists of repeating splendid examples of "that time, that place" from the past; antiquarian history involves honoring and preserving the precious heritage of our ancestors; and critical history seeks to liberate tormented elements of the past that still bear a grudge. By repeatedly summoning instances of "that time and that place" that have already passed, we use the past for our present life.

But enabling the past to serve life is not easy. If we fail to recall the past in time, we can quickly fall victim to the serious malady of taking history too seriously. As Nietzsche warned, an "excess of history is harmful to the living man."[3] Whether the history of a great hero, the history of our noble ancestors that we strive to preserve and protect, or the history of agonizing incidents that should never be repeated, we must "plasticize" ourselves, which requires tremendous capability.

> In order to determine this degree of history and, through that, the borderline at which the past must be forgotten if it is not to become the gravedigger of the present, we have to know precisely how great the *plastic force* of a person, a people, or a culture is. I mean that force of growing in a different way out of oneself, of reshaping and incorporating the past and the foreign, of healing wounds, compensating for what has been lost, rebuilding shattered forms out of one's self.[4]

Nietzsche, who valued a healthy life above all else, insists that one can live happily without remembering, but also stresses that life is impossible without the ability to forget. As he wrote, "No artist would achieve his picture, no field marshal his victory, and no people its freedom, without previously having desired and striven for them in that sort of unhistorical condition."[5] It is only humans who can constitute history, but without the ability to destroy what we have created, any possibility of life is annihilated. According to Nietzsche, the "animal, which is quite unhistorical and lives within a horizon which is almost a point, nevertheless is in a certain sense happy, or at least lives without boredom and dissimulation." In this context, animals' capacity to perceive

하나의 점과 같은 지평 속에 산다.” 동물은 비역사성을 원초적인 능력으로 가지고 있어서 “적어도 권태와 왜곡 없이 행복 속에 살아간다.” 그래서 니체는 동물이 가진 비역사성은 역사를 만들어내는 인간의 능력보다 더 중요하고 귀중한 원초적 능력이라고 본다.[6] 역사로부터 적절한 거리두기를 배우는 것은 건강한 삶을 위해 무엇보다 필요하다.

그러나 불러내고 싶지 않아도 끈질기게 따라붙는 ‘그때, 그곳’도 있다. 반복해서 꾸는 악몽처럼 시도 때도 없이 들러붙어 ‘그때, 그곳’의 끔찍한 기억을 불러내는 트라우마가 바로 그것이고, 끔찍하다고 할 수는 없지만, 저 구석 어딘가에 뾰족하게 자리하고 있는 물집이나 뾰루지처럼 성가시게 따라붙는 ‘그때, 그곳’도 있다. 또한 『잃어버린 시간을 찾아서』의 마들렌이 불러낸 유년 시절의 콩브레의 기억처럼, 어떤 사물에 의해 불현듯 불려 나오는 ‘그때, 그곳’도 있다. 무의식적으로 불려 나오는 ‘그때, 그곳’을 내 뜻대로 하기는 어려운 일이다.

그런데 니체의 말대로 동물은 완전히 비역사적이어서 ‘그때, 그곳’이 없는 것일까? 그렇지는 않을 것이다. 연어는 알을 낳기 위해 먼 바다에서 강을 거슬러 회귀하고, 비둘기는 자신의 집을 찾아가고, 철새들은 계절에 따라 자신이 살았던 곳으로 이주한다. 그들의 지평이 하나의 점이라면 어떻게 이들이 ‘그때, 그곳’으로 돌아갈 수 있겠는가? 그러나 우리는 동물을 본능에 새겨진 대로 반응할 뿐인 자동기계로 생각하기에 그들이 돌아가는 곳과 인간의 ‘그때, 그곳’은 아주 다르다고 여긴다. 인간에게 ‘그때, 그곳’은 특별한 이야기가 있는 곳이지만 동물에게는 그런 것이 있을 리 없다고 여기기 때문이다. 이런 점에서는 니체도 마찬가지였다. 하지만 그는 그것을 무능력으로 여기지 않고 오히려 건강한 삶을 위한 능력으로 여겼다.

생태철학자이자 동물행동학자인 쏨 반 두렌은 「도시의 펭귄들」이라는 글에서 꼬마펭귄이라 불리는 쇠푸른펭귄(Eudyptula minor)의 ‘그때, 그곳’을 이야기한다.[7] 꼬마펭귄은 체중이 1kg 남짓에 키는 30cm밖에 되지 않는 세상에서 가장 작은 펭귄종에 속한다. 이들은 번식지에 대한 강한 귀소성을 가지고 있어서 매년 자신이 최종적으로 번식한 장소를 찾아와 번식을 한다. 펭귄은 대부분의 삶을 물속에서 보내지만, 알을 낳고 품는 것은 뭍에서 한다. 그들의 뭍은 물과 땅이 만나는 축축한 해안이다. 펭귄의 습속은 바다가 주 생활 무대인 바다 거북이와도 다르고 갈매기와도 다르다. 바다 거북이는 1년에 단 하룻밤 해변에 올라와 알을 낳아 파묻고는 바다로 돌아가고, 갈매기는 바다 근처 높은 꼭대기에 둥지를 튼다. 그러나 멀리 날지 못하는 펭귄은 해안으로 나와서 바위틈에 굴을 파서 은신처를 만들고 알을 낳아 품는다. 알이 부화하고 병아리가 커서 다시 바다로 돌아갈 때까지 펭귄에게 해안은 또 다른 집이다.

호주 시드니항의 해안에는 해마다 꼬마펭귄이 번식을 위해 찾아온다. 50년 전만 해도 꼬마펭귄의 둥지는 시드니항 여기저기에서 쉽게 발견할 수 있었지만 지금은 아니다. 시드니항의 맨리 해변에는 아주 작은 규모의 펭귄 군집이 있을 뿐이고 이것은 호주 본섬에 남아있는 세 개의 군집 중 하나이다. 항구의 해안은 바다를 막아 만든 개인용 해수 풀장과 선착장을 위해 방파제가 빽빽하게 들어차 있어서 펭귄이

[6]
같은 책, 295.

[7]
Thom van Dooren, *Flight Ways: Life at the Edge of Extinction* (New York: Columbia University Press, 2014), 63–85.

[6]
Ibid., 295.

[7]
Thom van Dooren, *Flight Ways: Life and Loss at the Edge of Extinction* (New York: Columbia University Press, 2014), 63–85.

without history is more valuable and fundamental than humans' capacity to produce history.[6] Learning to keep a proper distance from history is essential to a healthy life.

And yet "that time, that place" endures, with or without our intention. It is like a trauma that clings to us, a recurring nightmare that stirs up terrible memories over and over again. While not necessarily agonizing, "that time, that place" is an annoying and persistent pain, like a blister or pimple on a part of our body that is usually forgotten or difficult to reach. In some cases, "that time, that place" can suddenly be called forth by an object or encounter, like the memories at Combray conjured by the taste of a madeleine in *In Search of Lost Time*. Because it can be evoked unconsciously, "that time, that place" is impossible for us to command.

But if animals are completely unhistorical, as Nietzsche surmised, does it mean that "that time, that place" do not exist for them? I don't believe this is true. Salmon return to their birthplace, arduously swimming from distant seas up rivers to lay their eggs. Pigeons always find their way home, and migratory birds travel thousands of miles to the same locations every year. If, as Nietzsche said, animals' "horizon is almost a point," then how can they return to "that time, that place"? Since we tend to regard animals as automata that simply respond to whatever is engraved in their instincts, we believe that the places to which they return must be inherently different from "that time, that place" of human life. For us, there is a special story attached to "that time, that place" but surely the same cannot be true for animals. Nietzsche himself followed this line of thought, even if he considered the animal perspective to be advantageous, rather than detrimental, for a healthy life.

In *Flight Ways: Life and Loss at the Edge of Extinction*, the philosopher, ethologist, and ecologist Thom van Dooren wrote about "that time, that place" of Eudyptula minor, or "little penguins."[7] Weighing just over a kilogram and measuring only 30 centimeters in height, little penguins are the world's smallest species of penguin. Although they spend most of their lives in the water, little penguins must return to the land each year to lay their eggs and rear their chicks. In fact, guided by their incredible homing instincts, little penguins return annually to the exact same breeding site, always located on a damp coastal area where the land meets the sea. Notably, the lives and habits of these penguins are very different from those of seagulls, sea turtles, or other animals that spend most of their lives in the ocean but breed on land. For example, sea turtles emerge from the water for just one night per year, crawling onto the beach to lay and bury their eggs, while seagulls make their nests high atop cliffs overlooking the sea. Since little penguins cannot fly, they climb up onto rocky shores and dig crevices between the rocks, where they then lay and incubate their eggs. They live on the shore until the eggs hatch and the chicks are grown, and then return to the sea.

Each year, little penguins return to lay their eggs on the shores of Sydney Harbour in Australia. Fifty years ago, the nests of little penguins were easy to find all over Sydney Harbour, but that is no longer the case. Today, there are only three remaining penguin colonies on mainland Australia, including a very small colony at Manly Beach in Sydney Harbour. Most of the pathways that the penguins once used to climb up to the shore have been blocked with breakwaters that were built to accommodate private seawater pools and marinas. The penguins' breeding cycle has been further disrupted by the noise and lights of the city. Even so, this small group of penguins stubbornly returns to Sydney Harbour every year, arduously clambering up the drainage channels in the

해안으로 올라갈 통로는 대부분 막혀 있다. 뿐만 아니라 도시의 소음과 불빛은 펭귄의 번식을 더욱 위태롭게 한다. 그러나 이 작은 체구의 펭귄들은 매년 시드니항을 찾아와 어떻게든 해안으로 접근한다. 심지어 방파제에 뚫린 배수로를 따라서라도 기어코 뭍으로 들어가고야 마는 것이다.

꼬마펭귄들이 이토록 고집스럽게 찾아가는 시드니항의 해안은 모두에게 무차별적인 환경이 아니라 야곱 폰 윅스킬이 말했던 꼬마펭귄의 움벨트(Umwelt)이다. 윅스킬은 유기체를 의미 있는 기호로 가득한 자신의 주변을 적극적으로 해석하는 생물학적인 주체로서 이해한다. 윅스킬에 따르면 모든 유기체는 자신의 고유한 움벨트를 가진다. 반 두렌은 이를 "이야기가 만들어진 장소"(storied-places)라고 부른다. 반 두렌은 이야기와 연대기를 구분하는데, 연대기는 사건들을 일어난 순서대로 단순히 나열하는 것이지만, 이야기는 맥락과 의미를 생성하는 방식으로 사건들이 짜여 들어가는 것이다. 그래서 장소는 단지 공간이 아니다. 장소를 만든다는 것은 어떤 공간을 물리적으로 바꾸는 것일 뿐 아니라 사회적이고 정신적인 과정을 통해 의미를 가지게 하는 것이다. 우리는 이를 인간에 국한된 능력이라고 여기지만 반 두렌은 시드니항의 꼬마펭귄들의 말해지지 않은 이야기를 듣기 위해 온 주의를 기울인다.

번식 장소에 대한 꼬마펭귄의 애착은 니체가 비판했던 역사의 과잉과 비슷해 보일 수 있다. 우리가 보기에 도시화된 시드니항은 더 이상 펭귄의 번식에 적합한 곳이 아니다. 그들은 과밀화된 해안의 가옥 밑이나 보트 밑에 굴을 파고 은신처를 만들었다가 둥지를 파괴당하고, 도시의 개와 고양이들에게 둥지를 습격당한다. 개체 수 급감의 가장 큰 원인은 이러한 번식 둥지의 유실이다. 이들을 세상 변한 줄도 모르고 하던 대로 하다가 죽어나가는 어리석은 동물이라 여길 수 있을 것이다.

그러나 반 두렌은 펭귄에게 번식 둥지는 하나의 서식지가 아니라 그들이 자신들의 경험으로부터 의미를 직조해 내는 "끝없이 이야기가 만들어진 장소"임을 강조한다. 꼬마펭귄의 번식을 위한 생태학적인 최적의 서식지는 너무 덥지 않고, 먹이를 구할 수 있는 곳과 가깝고, 물과 가까이 있으면서도 건조하고 안전한 은신처를 만들 수 있는 곳이다. 이런 최적의 서식지가 전혀 없는 것도 아니다. 그러나 이렇게 생태학적으로 최적이라고 생각되는 서식지도 꼬마펭귄이 집으로 선택하는 데 충분조건은 아니다. 실제 그런 장소 중 한 곳에는 단지 하나의 군집만 있거나 발견된 둥지가 하나뿐인 곳도 있었다. 펭귄의 역사와 이야기에는 생태학적인 요소들보다 더 많은 것들이 들어 있는 것 같다.

꼬마펭귄들이 번식지를 선택하는데 중요한 요소 중 하나는 지난 번식철에 만들었던 은신처에서 성공적으로 번식을 했는가 여부다. 이들은 지난 번식철에 성공적으로 새끼를 낳아 길렀던 특정한 장소에 큰 애착을 보이고 그곳을 다시 찾아 둥지도 다시 짓지 않고 쓰던 것을 그대로 쓴다. 이는 그들의 장소가 생태학적인 요인으로는 환원되지 않는 특별한 의미를 가진 '그때, 그곳'이라는 뜻이다. 주변에 동료 펭귄들이 많이 있는가도 이들이 은신처를 선택하는데 중요한 요소다. 그래서

breakwaters to make their way to shore.

Rather than an indiscriminate place for all, the shore of Sydney Harbour is the *"umwelt"* for the little penguins. This concept is borrowed from Jakob von Uexküll, who understood organisms as biological subjects that actively interpret their surroundings, which are imbued with meaningful signs. According to von Uexküll, every organism has its own umwelt, or to use van Dooren's term, "storied-place." Van Dooren distinguishes between chronology, a simple listing of events in the order in which they occurred, and story, a weaving of events in a way that creates context and meaning. In other words, a place is not just a geographical location. A place is created not only by physically changing a given location, but also by infusing it with meaning through various social and mental processes. Although most people seem to think that this ability is limited to humans, van Dooren draws our attention to the unspoken stories of the little penguins of Sydney Harbour.

The little penguins' attachment to their breeding ground might seem similar to the excess of history that Nietzsche warned against. From the human perspective, the urbanized Sydney Harbour is no longer a suitable breeding ground for the penguins, which are forced to dig burrows under houses or boats and to hide on overcrowded shores. The penguins and their nests also suffer periodic attacks from dogs and cats, which is a leading cause of their steep decline in their population. As such, it is easy for us to dismiss the little penguins as foolish creatures that keep doing the same things, even unto death, without realizing that the world has changed.

But as van Dooren stresses, breeding nests are not merely a habitat for the penguins, but a place woven with infinite stories that they use to derive meaning from their experiences. In terms of ecology, an optimal breeding site for little penguins should offer moderate temperatures, easy access to the water (where they can get food), and dry hidden spots where they can protect their chicks. Other such places can be found in Australia, but the little penguins have yet to seek them out. Indeed, one such site has only one colony of little penguins, or only one nest found. It seems that their story and history contains more than mere ecological conditions.

Little penguins prefer to breed in the exact same place that they bred in the previous year. Once they successfully breed and rear their chicks somewhere, they develop a strong attachment to the spot. They return to the same nest each year, which saves them the trouble of having to build a new one. In other words, the nest becomes "that time, that place" carrying a special meaning that cannot be reduced to ecological conditions. Another important factor in choosing a shelter is the presence of other little penguins in the vicinity. Thus, they look around the area and listen for familiar sounds, searching for a place where they will be surrounded by many friends. In fact, even if they have already built a nest, they might move it in order to be closer to their friends. Thus, for the little penguins, "that time, that place" is not frozen or petrified, but rather "a storied place where the values and importance that change throughout the penguin's life are remembered, reinterpreted and instilled."[8]

Three Types of "Here and Now"

Not that long ago, it was thought that the flow of time was equal and indiscriminate for everyone and everything. The modern representation of time consists of coordinates evenly spaced on a rectangular grid. In this conception of homogeneous time, nothing

주위를 둘러보고 소리를 듣고 친구들이 많은 곳을 택한다. 이미 둥지를 지었더라도 친구들이 많이 있는 곳으로 은신처를 옮기는 경우도 있다. 이처럼 꼬마펭귄의 '그때, 그곳'은 "펭귄의 생애를 통해서 변화하는 가치와 중요성이 기억되고, 재해석되고 불어넣어지는 이야기된 장소로 출현"하는 것이지 박제된 곳이 아니다.[8]

세 가지 종류의 '지금, 여기'

시간이 누구에게나 무엇에게나 무차별적으로 동일하게 흐르는 것으로 여겨진 것은 오래된 일이 아니다. 정방형의 공간에 시간의 좌표가 쭉 펼쳐져 있는 시간에 대한 표상은 근대의 발명품이다. 이렇게 균질적으로 펼쳐진 시간 속에서 현재는 과거와 미래의 경첩으로 작동할 뿐, 누구도 현재를 살지 못한다. 그래서 '지금, 여기'는 균질적이고 공허하게 흘러가는 시간의 톱니바퀴를 탈구 시켜 다른 시간, 다른 현재를 말하려는 용어이다. 그런데 거기에는 세 가지 서로 다른 '지금, 여기'가 있는 것처럼 보인다.

첫 번째는 고귀한 자의 "지금-여기"다. 「반시대적 고찰」에서 니체는 역사적 인간과 초역사적 인간을 이렇게 비교한다.[9] 누군가 이들에게 과거 10년, 20년을 다시 살고 싶은가를 묻는다면 그들은 아니라고 말할 것인데, 이유는 아주 다르다는 것이다. "역사적 인간은 과거로의 시선이 그들을 미래로 내몰고, 삶과 더 오래 겨루도록 그들의 용기를 북돋우고, 옳은 것은 앞으로 올 것이고 행복은 그들 앞에 가로놓인 산 뒤에 있다고 희망의 불을 지필 것"이기 때문이다. 역사적 인간에게 과거는 퇴보일 뿐이고 현재는 오직 미래를 위해서만 있을 뿐이다. 반면 "초역사적 인간은 과정 속에서 구원을 보지 않으며, 그에게 세상은 매 순간 완성되며 종말에 도달한다." 이들에게는 오직 매 순간 완성된 현재, '지금, 여기'만이 있을 뿐이기에 과거로 돌아갈 이유가 없다. 매 순간 충만한 "지금-여기"는 높은 수행의 경지에서나 경험할 수 있는 고귀한 자들의 시간이다. '지금, 여기'가 수행의 화두가 되는 것은 이 때문이다.

두 번째는 과거로부터 섬광처럼 오는 메시아적인 시간, "지금-여기"다. 「역사의 개념에 대하여」에서 벤야민은 인류의 진보라는 생각과 역사가 공허하고 균질적인 시간을 관통해서 진행한다는 근대의 시간성이 무관치 않음을 지적한다.[10] 역사는 통상 사건들이 시간의 순서로 쭉 나열되는 연대기적 서술 방식을 취하는데 이는 유기체가 성장의 단계를 순차적으로 밟아가는 것 같은 성장의 서사를 함의한다. 전진하는 역사의 기관차라는 역사주의에 대한 믿음은 맑스주의 역사유물론에서도 예외가 아니어서 역사유물론의 혁명은 모든 진보가 달성된 먼 미래에나 찾아오는 것이다. 그런데 벤야민은 이를 완전히 뒤집는다. 혁명은 전진하는 역사의 기관차를 정지시키는 것이고, 구원은 미래에 오는 것이 아니라 과거로부터 온다. 연대기적 역사는 승자의 기록이다. 그러나 거기에는 억압받고 배제되었던 수많은 자들의 삭제된 역사가 있다. "과거는 그것을 구원으로 지시하는 어떤 은밀한 지침을 지니고 있다."[11] 그는 삭제되었던 자들의 이야기를 되살리려 한다. 혁명은 이들 죽은 자들을 다시 불러일으키고, 산산이 부서진 것들을 다시 결합해서 그들의 세계를 드러내는

[8]
Ibid., 72.

[9]
니체, 『비극의 탄생/
반시대적 고찰』, 298.

[10]
발터 벤야민, 「역사의 개념에
대하여」, 『역사의 개념에
대하여/폭력비판을 위하여/
초현실주의 외』, 최성만
옮김(서울: 도서출판 길, 2009),
344.

[11]
같은 책, 331.

[9]
Nietzsche, *The Birth of Tragedy/ Thoughts Out of Season*, 298.

[10]
Walter Benjamin, "On the Concept of History" in *On the Concept of History/Toward the Critique of Violence/Surrealism*, trans. Choe Seong Man (Seoul: Gil, 2009), 344.

[11]
Ibid., 331.

[12]
Ibid., 345.

can exist in the present, which acts merely as a hinge between the past and future. Therefore, the "here and now" invokes a different time that appears through the disruption of this continuous, vacuous flow. Moreover, there are at least three different types of "here and now."

The first is the "here and now" of preeminent or enlightened people. In *Untimely Meditations*, Nietzsche compared "historical" and "suprahistorical" people, claiming that both types will say "no" when asked if they would like to relive the past ten or twenty years, but for very different reasons. For historical people, Nietzsche wrote, the past is only a regression and the present exists solely for the future. Thus, the "glance into the past pushes them into the future, fires their spirit to take up life for a longer time yet, kindles the hope that justice may still come and that happiness may sit behind the mountain towards which they are walking."[9] Suprahistorical people, on the other hand, are those who "do not see healing in the process and for whom the world is much more complete and at its end in every moment." Living purely in the present moment—the "here and now"—they have no reason to return to the past. This type of "here and now," marked by the fullness and perfection of each moment, is the state of the noblest people, which can only be attained through intensive discipline and meditation. Indeed, existing in the "here and now" has long been a primary aim of meditation.

The second type of "here and now" is the messianic time, which appears like a flash of light from the past. In "Theses on the Philosophy of History," Walter Benjamin points out that the idea of human progress is analogous to the modern temporality in which history proceeds through an empty, homogeneous time.[10] History typically arranges events in chronological order, implying a narrative of sequential progression, like an organism going through stages of growth. Marx's theory of historical materialism is no exception, viewing history as a locomotive with continuous forward motion and claiming that revolution will only come in the distant future after the fruition of progress. But Benjamin completely reverses this, asserting that revolution brings the locomotive of history to a halt, so that resurrection comes not from the future, but from the past: "The past carries a secret index with it, by which it is referred to its resurrection."[11] While the victors inevitably construct a chronological history, there is also an erased history of the countless who have been oppressed and excluded, which Benjamin attempts to revive. By assembling the shattered pieces of their stories and revealing their lives, he aims for a revolution that will awaken these dead. His term for the resurrection of the past, which stops the locomotive of history, is "*Jetztzeit*," or "here and now."[12]

The first two types of "here and now" are not readily accessible, being reached only through deep meditation or specific types of historical events. But the third "here and now" is always available to us, and can be easily attained within the time regulated by clocks. It is the time of daily life, although it is very different from the time of modernity. The third "here and now" is the time of the commune created through the meeting and interaction of different bodies.

For Immanuel Kant, time was an indiscriminate form of synthesis that made it possible to capture change, a concept that enabled the philosophical elucidation of modern science based on experiments. Similarly, industrial capitalism relied on clocks to regulate human bodies. In the early days of the Industrial Revolution, for example, British factories often disciplined their workers by hanging a clock in the work area.

것이다. 과거의 구원. 역사의 기관차를 멈춰 세우는 정지. 벤야민은 이를 "지금-시간"(Jetztzeit)이라 부른다.[12]

[12]
같은 책, 345.

[13]
이진경, 『코뮨주의: 공동성과 평등성의 존재론』(파주: 그린비, 2010) 참조.

앞의 두 가지 '지금, 여기'는 우리가 매번 경험할 수 있는 시간들이 아니다. 높은 수행의 경지에 올랐거나 역사적인 사건이 필요한 "지금-여기"이기 때문이다. 하지만 세 번째 '지금, 여기'는 우리에게 이미 와있는 "지금-여기"이지만 시계적 시간에 쉽게 탈취당하는 "지금-여기"다. 그것은 일상의 시간이지만 근대적 시간과는 아주 다른 시간으로 서로 다른 신체들이 만나고 섞이면서 만들어내는 코뮨적 시간으로서 "지금-여기"다.

칸트는 시간이 변화를 포착할 수 있게 해 주는 종합의 형식임을 철학적으로 개념화했다. 모든 것에게 무차별적으로 주어진다는 시간에 대한 이런 개념적 전제 덕분에 근대 실험과학은 철학적으로 해명될 수 있었다. 또한 산업자본주의는 시계를 신체를 규율하는 중요한 수단으로 사용했다. 산업혁명 초기 영국에서 노동자들을 규율하기 위해 가장 먼저 한 것이 공장에 시계를 걸어두는 일이었다는 것은 잘 알려진 이야기다. 그래서 근대적 시간성에 대한 가장 흔한 비판은 시간의 공간화, 즉 시간을 수치로 계량할 수 있는 것으로 만들었다는 것이다. 이 비판은 충분히 합당하지만 근대적 시간이 발명되기 전에도 양적인 것으로서의 시간이 없었던 것이 아니다.

근대 이전에도 일출과 일몰, 해가 가장 높이 뜨는 정오를 기준으로 하루의 시간을 가늠했고, 달의 모양에 따라 한 달의 시간을 가늠했다. 제사나 축제 등 모두가 한자리에 모이는 마을 행사가 열릴 수 있었던 것은 집단적으로 공유하는 시간성이 있었기 때문이다. 이는 인간에게만 국한되는 일이 아니었다. 꼬마펭귄이 번식철에 일제히 시드니항으로 돌아올 수 있는 것은 그들에게도 집단적으로 공유하는 시간성이 있기 때문이다. 그런데 이때 중요한 것은 언제 시작하고 언제 마치느냐와 같은 동시성이지 몇 시간 혹은 며칠 등의 시간의 양이 아니다. 그것은 모두 함께 무언가를 시작하고 끝을 내더라도 그 기간이 모두에게 균질하다는 전제는 없었다는 것을 의미한다.

이진경은 이러한 시간의 동시성을 서로 다른 반복 운동의 동조를 통해 설명하는 새로운 시간 개념을 제시한다.[13] 하지만 그는 후설처럼 상이한 시점에 속하는 것을 지금-시점으로 종합하기 위해 하나의 좌표계를 설정하지도 않고, 하이데거처럼 현존재의 일상을 위한 동일한 척도를 가정하는 세계시간을 설정하지도 않는다. 이진경에 따르면, 시간이란 상이한 신체들의 운동이 '리듬적 종합'을 이룬 결과이다. 살아있는 것들이 무언가를 함께하기 위해서는 시점의 동기화(synchronization)가 필요하다. 그러나 동기화를 위한 척도가 미리 있는 것은 아니고, 하나만 있는 것도 아니다. 물론 시점의 동기화를 위해 해와 달의 순환적 반복 운동이 중요한 기준이 되는 것은 사실이고 칸트의 시간 개념도 지구의 자전운동이라는 경험을 바탕으로 그것을 추상화해낸 것이다. 그러나 그 순환적 반복의 가치와 중요성은 생물종마다, 집단마다, 심지어 동종 내에서는 지역마다 처한 상황마다 모두 상이하다. 이것이 집합체마다 상이한 리듬적 종합이 발생하는 이유다.

유기체가 생물학적으로 시간을 감각하는 생체시계는 해와 달의 운동 패턴뿐

기념하다, 함께-기억하다

[13]
Yi-Jinkyung, *Commune-ism: The Ontology of Communality and Equality* (Seoul: Greenbee, 2010).

The most common criticism of modern temporality is that it spatializes time, making it numerically quantifiable. While this criticism seems reasonable enough, the notion of time as a quantifiable entity certainly existed prior to the modern era.

Long before modernity, the time of day was determined by the trajectory of the sun, while the months were charted by the shape of the moon. This shared temporality is what allowed early people to gather together for village ceremonies and festivals. But of course, such events are not limited to humans. The fact that little penguins return in unison to Sydney Harbour during breeding season clearly demonstrates that they also share a collective time. What matters here is not the duration in hours or days of the event, but the simultaneity of the start and end points. Thus, even if every participant started and ended the event at the same time, there is no way of knowing that the duration was the same for all.

In his book *Commune-ism*, Yi-Jinkyung proposed a new concept of time in which he attempted to explain this simultaneity through the synchronization of various repetitive movements.[13] Notably, however, Yi does not try to synthesize different eras within the present by establishing a single coordinate system, like Edmund Husserl, or a world time based on the standard of "Dasein" ("there-being"), like Martin Heidegger. Instead, Yi posits time as the result of the rhythmic synthesis of the movements of different bodies. In order for living beings to do anything together, the synchronization of time is required. But there are seemingly infinite possible standards for establishing such synchronization, none of which are determined in advance. Of course, the cyclical motion of the sun and moon are crucial criteria for the synchronization of time, and Kant also attempted to make time abstract based on our experience of the earth's rotation. However, the value and importance of this cyclical repetition differs from species to species, and also varies within species depending on the group or region. Thus, different rhythmic syntheses occur in different aggregates.

Every organism also senses time via a biological clock, which is a rhythmic synthesis based not only on the movements of the sun and moon, but also on the repetitive movements of its own unique genetic pattern of cells. But this sense of time extends beyond the individual organism. In order to farm, a farmer must synchronize his body with the movements of the sun and the rhythm of the soil, water, seeds, plants, and insects. Thus, the time of all of these entities is synchronized. This is not only true for humans, as a bee also cannot survive without adapting itself to the rhythms of the sun, moon, and flowers. The bee's body evolved according to these rhythms. Indeed, every being lives and dies depending on every other being. Our bodies evolved to adapt to the rhythms of the beings and situations on which we depend, and our time arises and disappears in rhythmic synchronizations with other beings on various scales.

Yi-Jinkyung calls these aggregates of rhythmic synchronization "communes," which is a community of members whose mutual relationships are a gift to one another. In accordance with Spinoza, who argued that an individual is not an indivisible entity with a fixed boundary, but rather something with a consistent ratio of motion and rest, each commune is an individual and a body moving with the same rhythm. But this notion of a body moving in rhythm should not arouse thoughts of totalitarianism, since no body is a single commune. Every individual is a multiplicity of numerous communes that is continuously reconstructed as they appear and disappear. When some form of rhythmic synchronization occurs, a commune is created, as is its time, or "here and now."

아니라 자신을 구성하는 유전적으로 상이한 세포들의 집합이 세대를 거쳐 가며 만들어낸 운동의 반복 패턴이 한데 묶이면서 종합된 리듬적 종합의 결과다. 생물학적 시간만 그런 것이 아니다. 농부는 해의 운동 리듬과 작물과 토양과 물과 주변 곤충들의 생장 리듬에 자신의 신체를 동조시키지 않으면 농사를 지을 수 없다. 그들의 시간은 이러한 동기화 속에서 발생한다. 사람만 그런 것이 아니다. 가령, 벌은 해와 달의 리듬뿐 아니라 주변 꽃들의 생장 리듬에 자신을 맞추지 않으면 살아갈 수 없고, 그의 신체는 그 리듬에 맞추어져 진화되었다. 살아있는 모든 것은 다른 것에 기대어 살고 죽는다. 그래서 그들의 신체는 자신들이 기대고 있는 것들의 리듬에 맞출 수 있는 능력을 가지는 방향으로 진화되었고 그들의 시간은 다양한 스케일에서 다양한 자들과의 리듬적 동조들 속에서 발생하고 사라진다.

이렇게 리듬적 동조를 이루어내는 집합체들을 이진경은 공동체, 서로에게 선물이 되는 관계를 의미하는 코뮌(commune)이라 부른다. 더 이상 분할할 수 없는 고정된 경계를 가진 것이 개체가 아니라 동일한 운동과 정지의 비율을 가지는 것은 무엇이든 하나의 개체라고 했던 스피노자를 참조한다면 코뮌은 하나의 개체, 동일한 리듬으로 운동하는 하나의 신체라고 할 수 있을 것이다. 하나의 리듬으로 운동하는 신체라고 해서 곧바로 전체주의를 떠올리지는 마시라. 우리의 신체조차도 단 하나의 코뮌이 아니다. 하나의 개체조차도 수많은 코뮌들의 다양체이고, 그것은 생성 소멸하면서 끊임없이 재구성된다. 리듬적 동조를 통해 하나의 코뮌이 만들어지면 그때 그들의 시간이 발생한다. 그것은 코뮌적 시간인 '지금, 여기'이다.

코뮌적 시간으로서 '지금, 여기'는 높은 수행을 통해서만 체험할 수 있는 것도 아니고 혁명의 순간에만 체험되는 것도 아니다. 오히려 이렇게 말해야 한다. '지금, 여기'는 누군가/무언가와 함께하는 어디에나 있다. 그러나 '지금, 여기'는 영원히 지속되지 않는다. 그것은 코뮌을 형성할 때 생기고, 코뮌이 해체될 때 사라지는 것이기 때문이다. 서로 다른 코뮌들의 복잡하게 얽혀 있는 세계가 단일한 척도의 시간을 가진다는 것은 이치에 맞지 않는다. 우리에게는 우리가 구성하고 또 구성 요소로 엮여 들어간 수많은 코뮌들이 있고 그 코뮌들의 수만큼 복수의 '지금, 여기'들이 있다. 이 "지금-여기"들은 인간만이 아니라 복수종(multispecies)과 함께 구성된 코뮌적 시간이다.

그러므로 코뮌적 시간, "지금, 여기'는 "끔찍한 과거 혹은 에덴동산 같은 과거와 종말론적인 미래 혹은 구원을 약속하는 미래 사이에서 사라져 버리는 회전축으로서"의 현재가 아니라 "수많은 장소와 시간, 수많은 문제와 의미의 무한연쇄에 얽혀 있는 죽을 운명의" 비인간과 인간이 살고 죽는 "두터운 현재(thick present)이다.[14] 누구도 무엇도 단 하나의 코뮌에만 속해 있지 않다. 우리 모두는 복수의 "지금-여기"들이 중첩된 두터운 현재를 산다.

두터운 현재인 "지금-여기"는 안전한 미래를 위해 위험을 피하는 시간이 아니라 위험과 마주하면서 "트러블과 함께 하는" 시간이다. 해러웨이는 'trouble'이란 말에는 불러일으키다, 애매하게 만들다, 방해하다는 의미가 있음을 상기시킨다.[15] 트러블과

[14]
도나 해러웨이, 『트러블과 함께하기: 자식이 아니라 친척을 만들자』, 최유미 옮김(서울: 마농지, 2021), 8.

[15]
같은 책, 7.

[14]
Donna Haraway, *Staying with the Trouble: Making Kin in the Chthulucene*, trans. Choi Yumi (Seoul: Manongji, 2021), 8.

[15]
Ibid., 7.

[16]
Ibid., 47.

[17]
van Dooren, *Flight Ways: Life and Loss at the Edge of Extinction*, 63.

This "here and now" as the time of a commune does not require intensive training, nor does it exist only at the moment of revolution. On the contrary, this "here and now" is always there, but it does not last forever. It appears when the commune is formed and disappears when the commune is disbanded. It does not make sense for a world of intricately intertwined communes to abide by a single time scale. Each of us has woven ourselves into numerous communes, and for each of these communes, there is a "here and now." Of course, these instances of "here and now" extend beyond the human realm to include many other species and beings.

For Donna Haraway, the "here and now" of the commune is not the present as "a vanishing pivot between awful or edenic pasts and apocalyptic or salvific futures." Instead, it is a "thick present," where non-humans and humans live and die, "as mortal critters entwined in myriad unfinished configurations of places, times, matters, meanings."[14] No one and nothing belongs to just one commune. We all live in a thick present of superimposed layers of "here and now."

For Haraway, this "thick present" is not a time to avoid risk in order to ensure a safe future, but rather a time to "stay with the trouble." As she reminds us, the word "trouble" can also mean to evoke, obscure, or obstruct.[15] Thus, staying with the trouble means obstructing the temptation to erase the past and present in the name of the future, obscuring easy solutions, and evoking responses to those who are facing the "here and now." This form of "here and now" is the time to discover and nurture invisible communes that we did not even know we were depending on, the time to learn to synchronize with the rhythms of others, and the time to develop our "response-ability."

Remember and Re-member

To remember is to "re-member," or to once again become a member.[16] In the case of the little penguins, memories of their breeding grounds are passed down through the generations. After the young chicks grow up, they return each year to the same place where they were born to breed their own chicks. Inheriting these memories, they return annually to their birthplace to once again become a commune member (to "re-member"). Their time on land is very different from their time in the water. As such, the penguins live in a "thick present" woven with many different versions of "here and now."

But now because of human activities, their breeding grounds are endangered. Their access to the shore has been blocked, their breeding habits are threatened by the bright lights and noises of cars, they have been attacked by dogs and cats (sometimes purposely released), and even shot by people angered by the noise of their mating calls. If the breeding grounds disappear, so will the continuity of the penguins' lives. Even so, the little penguins seem very reluctant to change their behavior or their valuation of their shelters on Manly Beach. In the epigraph of van Dooren's book, he quotes ornithologist Chris Challies, who said, "Little penguins are extremely robust both mentally and physically, and when confronted with human activities, even if adverse, they are unyielding."[17]

The world is now filled with humans and non-humans who have been deprived of their "storied places." Communes and times that have been passed down for many generations are being destroyed for reasons related to the market, development, energy consumption, urban renewal, or even environmental conservation. These are places

함께하기는 미래를 위한다는 명목으로 과거와 현재를 모두 지워버리려는 유혹을 방해하고 손쉬운 해결책을 애매하게 만들고 "지금-여기" 마주하고 있는 자들에 대한 응답을 불러일으키는 것이다. 코뮨적 시간, '지금, 여기'는 자신이 기대고 있는 줄도 몰랐던, 보이지 않던 코뮨들을 발견하는 시간이고, 그것들을 돌보는 시간이고, 다른 자들의 리듬에 동조되기를 배우는 시간, 그것으로부터 응답-능력을 키우는 시간이다.

[16]
같은 책, 47.

[17]
van Dooren, *Flight Ways: Life and Loss at the Edge of Extinction*, 63.

기억하다. 다시 멤버가 된다.

'기억하다'는 '다시 멤버가 되는 것'(re-member)이다.[16] 꼬마펭귄에게 번식지에 대한 기억은 세대를 걸쳐서 이어진다. 어린 것들이 자라 번식철이 되면 자신이 태어났던 곳으로 돌아가서 번식을 한다. 이들은 자신들이 태어났고 새끼를 낳았던 그들의 장소, 그들이 생명을 얻었던 코뮨에 대한 기억을 계승하고, 그 코뮨에 다시 멤버가 되기 위해 돌아온다. 뭍으로 돌아온 그들의 시간은 물속에서의 시간과는 아주 다른 시간일 것이다. 펭귄들은 서로 다른 '지금, 여기'들을 넘나드는 두터운 현재를 산다.

인간들의 활동 때문에 그들의 번식 장소는 위험에 처해있다. 그들은 해안을 봉쇄당했고, 짝을 구하는 밤의 울음소리가 시끄럽다고 무자비하게 총질을 당하기도 했고, 고의로 혹은 부주의로 풀어놓은 개들과 고양이들에게 습격을 당하기도 했고, 너무 강한 자동차 불빛 때문에 번식이 실패로 돌아가기도 했다. 펭귄들의 번식 장소가 사라지면 이들의 계속성도 사라질 것이다. 그러나 꼬마펭귄들은 맨리 해안의 여러 은신처들에 대한 자신들의 가치와 의미를 좀처럼 바꾸지 않는다. 반 두렌은 「도시의 펭귄들」의 제사(epigraph)에서 번식지에 대한 펭귄의 확고한 애착을 크리스 찰리스를 인용해서 이렇게 쓴다. "펭귄은 신체적으로 정신적으로 극도로 강건하다. 그들이 인간의 활동과 마주했을 때, 그것이 비록 자신들에게 적대적인 경우에조차, 그들은 결코 포기하지 않는다."[17]

지금 지구상에는 자신들의 "이야기가 만들어진 장소"를 빼앗긴 인간과 인간 아닌 자들이 넘쳐난다. 시장을 위해, 개발을 위해서, 더 많은 에너지를 위해, 도시 재정비를 위해, 심지어 환경보호를 위해, 혹은 전쟁 같은 폭력적인 사태 때문에 세대를 이어 살아온 그들의 코뮨들, 그들의 시간들이 파괴되고 있다. 그곳은 그들 코뮨들의 고유한 시간이 있는 곳이고, 그들이 다시 멤버가 되는 장소이자 그들의 계속성을 이어가는 곳이고, 그로부터 그들의 '지금, 여기'가 구성되는 곳이다. 코뮨이 작동해서 공동의 리듬을 만든다는 것은 서로가 서로에게 빚져 사는 무구하지 않은 관계를 서로가 서로에게 선물이 되도록 서로를 적극적으로 돌본다는 의미이다. 이러한 코뮨들이, 그들의 장소들이 지금 위기에 처해 있다.

하지만 우리는 더 좋은 환경, 더 좋은 자원이 제공되면 이야기가 만들어진 장소를 잃은 비인간/인간들의 고통이 해결될 수 있을 것이라 여긴다. 그들의 장소를 복구하는 대신 "자연 친화"적인 동물원에 몰아넣으면 해결된다고 생각하고, 돈으로 보상해주면 그만이라 생각하는 것이다. 하지만 이야기가 만들어진 장소는 단지 점유되었던 공간도 아니고 쉽게 바꿀 수 있는 공간도 아니다. 반 두렌이 말하는 것처럼, 들리지 않았던

[18]
Ibid., 79.

[19]
Haraway, *Staying with the Trouble: Making Kin in the Chthulucene*, 72.

[20]
Ibid., 47.

where communes have their own time, where they re-member, where they retain their continuity, and where they constitute their "here and now." When a commune works and creates a shared rhythm, the members must actively take care of one another in order to ensure that their relationship, even if it is not necessarily amiable, is a gift. These communes and their places are now in crisis.

But we think the suffering of non-humans/humans who lost these storied places will be solved if we make a greater effort to improve the environment and resources. Too often, instead of trying to restore these places, we settle for makeshift solutions, such as putting animals in "cageless" zoos or offering financial compensation. But storied places are much more than simple habitats, and are thus not so easy to replace. We must train our ears to listen carefully to the stories we have not heard, or the stories we did not want to hear. We should recall the words of philosopher and eco-feminist Val Plumwood, who declared that the recognition of "earth others as fellow agents and narrative subjects is crucial for all ethical, collaborative, communicative and mutualistic projects."[18] Attuning ourselves to different stories can change our ethics and "response-ability."

We now live in a world in which many beings are vanishing every day. Of course, everything that is created must eventually disappear, but too many beings, both human and non-human, are disappearing too quickly for us to continue to justify the cost of our comfortable and convenient urban lives. Due to our insensitivity and inability to synchronize with their rhythm, these beings are losing the times of "here and now" that they created by interacting with other bodies. We must mourn this loss. As van Dooren said, "Mourning is about dwelling with a loss and so coming to appreciate what it means, how the world has changed, and how we must ourselves change and renew our relationships if we are to move forward from here."[19]

Haraway further reminds us that to "commemorate" is to "com-memorate," or to remember together. By remembering together, we can begin to entice and extend the communes that will disappear unless their participants can again become a member in the embodied present. Com-memorating is "actively repeating, reviving, taking again, and recovering."[20] If art is a monument, a condensation of our response-ability and affect, then let's produce monuments that bring "that time and that place," as created through the interaction of both human and more-than-human beings, into the "here and now," helping us to restore our senses and again become members with them.

이야기, 아니 들으려 하지 않았던 이야기에 귀를 기울이고 그것을 듣기 위해 우리의 감각을 단련시키는 일이 필요하다. 페미니스트 생태 철학자 발 플럼우드가 말한 것처럼 "지구의 타자들을 동료 행위자로, 서사의 주체로 인식하는 것은 윤리적이고 협동적이고 소통적이고 상호적인 모든 기획에서 결정적이다."[18] 이야기가 달라지면 우리의 윤리와 응답-능력(response-ability)은 달라질 수 있다.

지금 우리는 많은 것들이 사라져가는 세계에 산다. 생겨난 것이 사라지는 것이야 당연한 일이지만, 안락하고 편리한 도시의 삶을 위해 너무 많은 인간 이상의 존재들이 너무도 급속하게 세상에서 사라져가고 있다. 그들의 리듬과 동조되지 못하는 우리의 무능력과 무감각으로 인해 그들이 다른 신체들과 섞이며 지금까지 만들어온 "지금-여기"의 시간들을 상실하고 있는 것이다. 우리는 이 상실을 애도해야 한다. 반 두렌은 "애도란 상실과 함께 사는 것이고, 그래서 상실이 의미하는 게 무엇인지, 세계가 어떻게 변했는지, 그리고 우리가 여기서 앞으로 나아가야 한다면 우리 자신이 어떻게 변해서 우리의 관계들을 어떻게 새롭게 해야 하는지를 잘 인식하게 되는 것과 관련이 있다"[19] 고 쓴다.

'기념하다'는 '함께 기억하다'(com-memorate)이다. 기념한다는 것은 적극적으로 다시 멤버가 되지 않으면 사라질 무엇을 육화된 현재 속으로 유인하고 연장하기 위해 함께 기억하는 것이다. 그것은 "적극적으로 반복하기, 되살아나기, 다시 취하기, 회복하기"이다.[20] 예술이 감응으로 응결된 기념비라면, 나는 인간 이상의 존재들이 서로의 신체를 섞으면서 만들어온 '그때, 그곳'을 '지금, 여기'로 데려와서 우리의 감각을 다시 만들고, 우리도 그들과 다시 멤버가 되게 할 그런 기념비들을 보고 싶다.

[18]
Ibid., 79.

[19]
해러웨이, 『트러블과 함께하기: 자식이 아니라 친척을 만들자』, 72.

[20]
같은 책, 47.

나너의 기억   My Your Memory

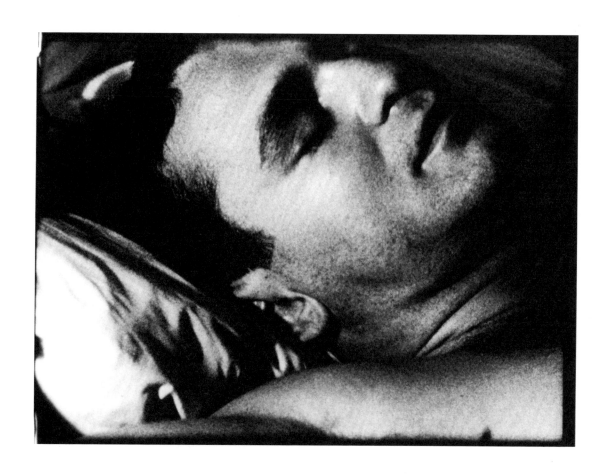

앤디 워홀, ‹수면›, 1963,
16mm 필름을 디지털 파일로
변환, 흑백, 무음, 5시간 21분.
앤디워홀뮤지엄(피츠버그) 소장.
앤디워홀재단 제공.

Andy Warhol, *Sleep*, 1963,
16mm film transferred to
digital file, black-and-white,
silent, 5 hrs. 21 min. Collection
of The Andy Warhol Museum,
Pittsburgh. Contribution to The
Andy Warhol Foundation for
the Visual Arts. Inc.

나너의 기억

visualization mode 141　_corneal radius +% : 669

[1235,
[1259
[1253,

나너의 기억

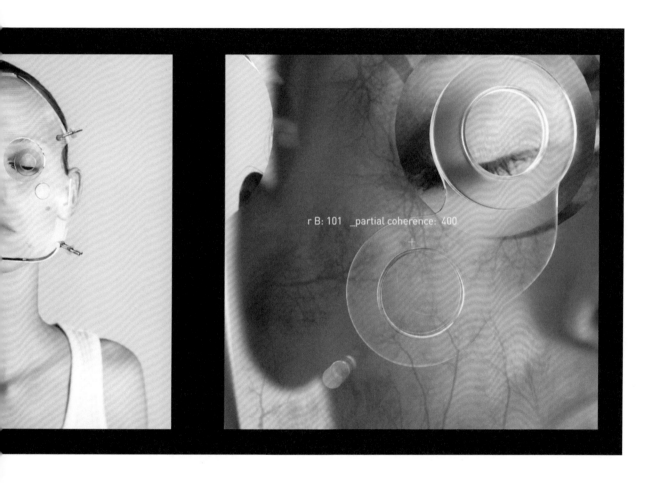

허만 콜겐, ‹망막›, 2018,
3채널 비디오, 컬러, 사운드,
2채널 오디오, 레이저, 10분.
작가 소장. 파라다이스
아트스페이스 공동 제작.

Herman Kolgen, *RETINA*, 2018,
three-channel video, color,
sound, two-channel audio, laser,
10 min. Courtesy of the artist.
Co-produced with Paradise Art
Space.

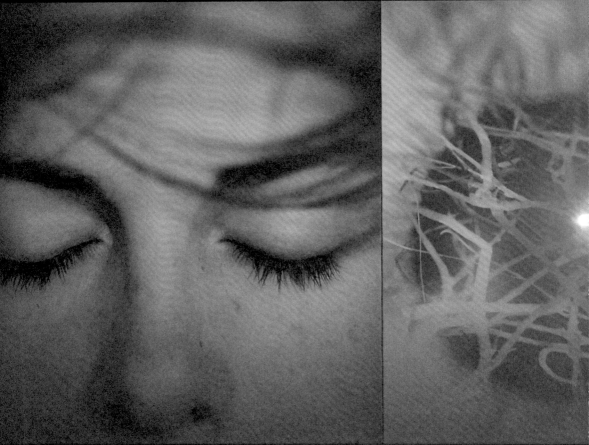

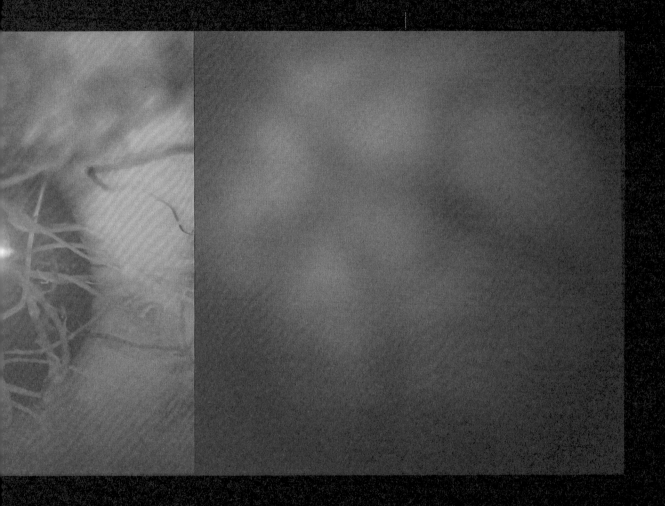

양정욱, ‹피곤은 언제나 꿈과
함께›, 2013, 나무, 모터, 실,
백열등, 아크릴, 플라스틱
병, 300×197×197cm.
국립현대미술관 소장.

Yang Junguk, *Fatigue
Always Comes with a Dream*,
2013, wood, motor, thread,
lamp, acrylic, plastic bottle,
300×197×197cm. MMCA
collection.

나너의 기억

나녀의 기억

임윤경, ‹Q&A›, 2016, 영상
설치: 2채널 비디오, 컬러,
사운드, 14분 36초; 전시
부스, 145×300×300cm.
국립현대미술관 소장.

Lim Yoonkyung, *Q&A*, 2016,
video installation: two-channel
video, color, sound, 14 min.
36 sec.; exhibition booth,
145×300×300cm. MMCA
collection.

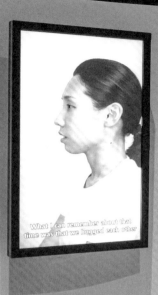

What I can remember about that time was that we hugged each other

나너의 기억

지금, 여기

Here and Now

세실리아 비쿠냐, ‹나의 베트남
이야기›, 2021, 단채널 비디오,
컬러, 사운드, 6분 45초.
세실리아 비쿠냐, 라 카사 데
라스 레코히다스 및 리만머핀
뉴욕/홍콩/서울/런던 제공.

제13회 광주비엔날레
«떠오르는 마음, 맞이하는 영혼»
지원으로 제작.

— 촬영 및 편집:
   프란시스카 베니테스
— 시낭독: 세실리아 비쿠냐
— 퍼포먼스: 라 카사 데 라스
   레코히다스, 2020
— 푸티지 제공: 벤자민 맷

Cecilia Vicuña, *My Vietnam
Story*, 2021, single-channel
video, color, sound, 6 min. 45
sec. Courtesy of Cecilia Vicuña,
La Casa de las Recogidas and
Lehmann Maupin, New York,
Hong Kong, Seoul and London.

Video created on the occasion of
"Minds Rising, Spirits Tuning:
13th Gwangju Biennale,"
South Korea.

— Camera and editing by
   Francisca Benítez
— Poem song by Cecilia
   Vicuña
— Performance by La Casa de
   las Recogidas, 2020
— Footage by Benjamin Matte

〈나의 베트남 이야기〉는 사라져버린 세계를
위한 애도의 움직임이다. 자국의 독립과
주권을 위해 싸운 베트남 소녀들의 열정과
헌신은 나에게 가슴 깊은 감동을 주었다.
이것이 바로 내가 이 작업을 만든 이유이고
작업을 기억할 때마다 눈물짓게 되는 이유다.
내가 칠레에서 만났던 베트남 소녀들은
타인에게 자신의 인생을 바치며 느끼는
생경한 기쁨에 빛났으며 벅차있었다. 나는
이전까지 이런 걸 경험해 본 적 없었다. 미국
영화의 무상한 활기참이나 로맨스 소설을
읽고 사랑을 찾는 것이 유일한 바램인 칠레의
청소년들과는 상반되는 기쁨이었다. 그들의
깨달음은 나의 인생을 일깨워 주었다. 그들이
앞서 겪은 후 나에게 알려준 가르침은 그들의
세계가 파괴되었던 것과 같은 방식으로
우리의 현실, 그러니까 칠레의 사회도 파괴될
수 있다는 것이었다. 나에게 이 작업은 무장
투쟁을 옹호하기 위한 것이 아니라, 타인을
사랑하라는 아주 오래된 가르침을 전하기
위해 헌신하는 이들을 찬양하기 위한 것이다.

My Vietnam Story is an act of mourning for a
disappeared world. The fervor and devotion
with which the Vietnamese girls fought for
their independence and autonomy touched
my heart in its deepest place. That is why
I made these works. That is why I cry each
time I remember it. The Vietnamese girls I
met in Chile blossomed, illuminated by a
strange kind of joy: the joy of giving your
life for others. It was something I had never
experienced before. A joy so contrary to the
vacuous cheerfulness of American movies,
or of the Chilean teenagers whose only
aspiration was to read romantic novels and
find love. Their enlightenment enlightened
my life. The anticipatory knowledge they
shared with me made me understand that our
reality, our Chilean world, could be destroyed
the same way theirs was destroyed. For me,
this is not a work in praise of armed struggle,
but a celebration of giving yourself to the
transmission of an ancient knowledge: love for
others.

Here and Now

시프리앙 가이야르, ‹호수 아치›,
2007, 단채널 비디오, 컬러, 무음,
1분 43초. 국립현대미술관 소장.

Cyprien Gaillard, *The Lake
Arches*, 2007, single-channel
video, color, silent, 1 min. 43 sec.
MMCA collection.

지금, 여기

Here and Now

지금, 여기

아크람 자타리, ‹스크립트›,
2018, 단채널 비디오, 컬러,
사운드, 7분 24초. ⓒ 아크람
자타리, 토마스데인갤러리 제공.

Akram Zaatari, *The Script*, 2018,
single-channel video, color,
sound, 7 min. 24 sec. ⓒ Akram
Zaatari, Courtesy of the artist and
Thomas Dane Gallery.

지금, 여기

〈스크립트〉는 이슬람 전통 기도 의식을
수행하는 아버지와 그를 방해하려 하는
어린 아들의 모습을 보여준다. 이 작품은
유튜버들이 온라인에 업로드 한 수많은
영상들을 참조하여 제작되었다. 유튜브에서
수집한 짧은 영상들은 대부분 화질이 낮은
휴대폰 카메라로 어떠한 편집도 없이 한
번에 촬영되어 업로드 된다. 〈스크립트〉는
이 같은 아이디어를 차용하여 작품의
'대본'(스크립트)으로 사용한다.

아랍어로 기도를 뜻하는 '살라트'는
요가의 기본 동작과 비슷하게 바닥에
엎드리는 일종의 절 동작을 바탕으로 한다.
살라트는 하루에 다섯 번씩 수행되어야 하고,
정해진 규범 안에서 엄격하게 통제된 정도의
변형만이 허용된다.

영상 속에서 아버지는 두 번의 기도를
수행한다. 첫 번째 기도는 그의 가정집을
배경으로 규범에 맞추어 수행되고,
무대에서의 두 번째 기도는 변형된 형식으로
수행된다. 이 변형된 형식은 아버지가 그의
작은 아들이 기도 의식을 장난처럼 즐기고
있는 것을 알아채고 나서 절을 반복하는
것이다.

The Script is based on many videos uploaded
by Youtubers online, showing a father praying
in the muslim tradition, while a child, his son,
tries to distract him. These short videos are
often taken with lowers cellphone cameras
in single-unedited-shots and uploaded onto
YouTube. *The Script*, restages the same idea
and uses it as a script (therefore the title) for an
art video.

"Salaat" [prayer in Arabic], is based on
a set of prostrations very similar to basic yoga
moves accompanied by prayer. They are to be
performed five times a day and represent strict
variations on the same protocol.

In *The Script*, the father performs his
prayer twice. The first prayer is performed
unchanged, in a home setup, whereas
the second time is performed on stage
with uncommon variations. In the second
performance the father allows himself to
repeat continuous prostrations when he
realizes that his younger son is enjoying it.

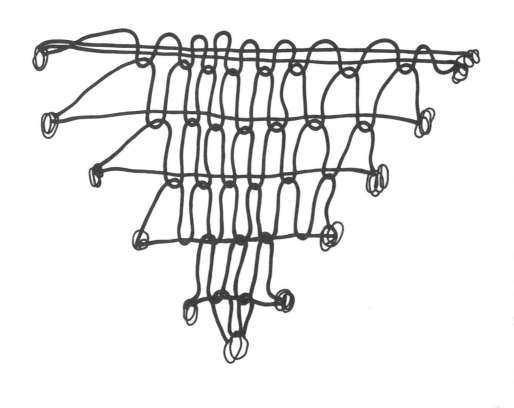

루이즈 부르주아, <코바늘 III>,
1998, 믹소그라피, 71.1×84.8cm.
국립현대미술관 소장.
© The Easton Foundation/VAGA
at ARS, New York/SACK,
Seoul, 2022.

Louise Bourgeois, *Crochet III*,
1998, mixography, 71.1×84.8cm.
MMCA Collection. © The Easton
Foundation/VAGA at ARS,
New York/SACK, Seoul, 2022.

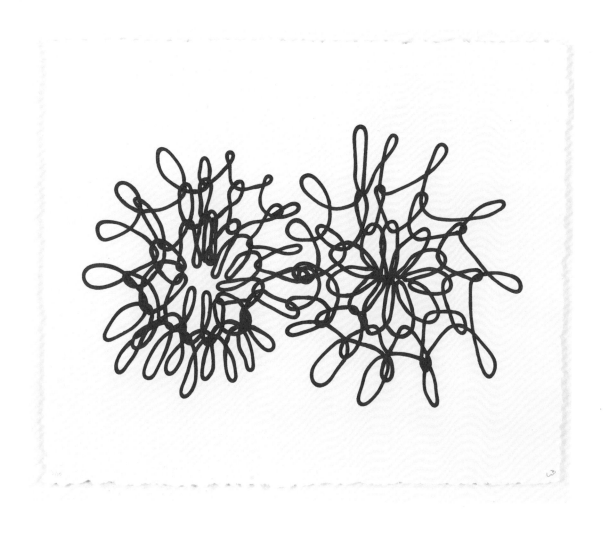

루이즈 부르주아, 〈코바늘 IV〉,
1998, 믹소그라피, 71.1×84.8cm.
국립현대미술관 소장.
© The Easton Foundation/VAGA
at ARS, New York/SACK,
Seoul, 2022.

Louise Bourgeois, *Crochet IV*
1998, mixography, 71.1×84.8cm.
MMCA Collection. © The Easton
Foundation/VAGA at ARS,
New York/SACK, Seoul, 2022.

그때, 그곳   That Time, That Place

안리 살라, ⟨붉은색 없는 1395일⟩,
2011, 단채널 HD 비디오, 컬러,
5.0 서라운드 사운드, 43분 46초.
마리안굿맨갤러리, 하우저&워스
제공. ⓒ 안리 살라, 에스에즐라
카메릭, 아트앤젤, SCCA/2011.

— 영상 제작: 리리아
  베지이자와의 협력
— 영상 프로젝트: 에스에즐라
  카메릭, 안리 살라(제작),
  아리 벤자민 마이어스(협력)

Anri Sala, *1395 Days Without
Red*, 2011, single-channel HD
video, color, 5.0 surround sound,
43 min. 46 sec. Courtesy: Marian
Goodman Gallery, Hauser
& Wirth. ⓒ Anri Sala, Šejla
Kamerić, Artangel, SCCA/2011.

— In collaboration with Liria
  Begeja, From a project by
  Šejla Kamerić and Anri
  Sala in collaboration with
  Ari Benjamin Meyers.

그때, 그곳

That Time, That Place

That Time, That Place

그때, 그곳

송주원, ‹뾰루지.물집.사마귀.점›,
2021, 3채널 HD 비디오, 컬러,
사운드, 7분 15초. 작가 소장.

— 감독: 송주원
— 안무: 송주원
— 협력안무 및 퍼포머:
   공영선, 김호연, 나연우,
   이주성, 임진호
— 퍼포먼스 크리에이티브
   프로듀서: 김서령, 이동민
— 프로젝트 매니저: 이경미
— 촬영 감독: 최용석
— A카메라: 황호규
— 편집: 최이다, 문준영
— 색보정: 한동균
— 사운드: 홍초선
— 사운드 기록: 곽소민
— 스크립터: 김민경
— 자문: 임인자
— 사진: 김정엽
— 광주 코디네이터: 도민주
— 후원: 와우책문화예술센터,
   서서울미술관
— 제작: 일일댄스프로젝트

Song Joowon, *Pimple.Blister.
Wart.Mole*, 2021, three-channel
HD video, color, sound, 7 min.
15 sec. Courtesy of the artist.

— Director: Song Joowon
— Choreography: Song
   Joowon
— Co Choreography and
   Performer: Kong Youngsun,
   Kim Hoyeun, Na Yeonwoo,
   Lee Jusung, Lim Jinho
— Performance Creative
   Producer: Kim Seoryoung,
   Lee Dongmin
— Project Manager: Lee Mia
   Kyoungmi
— D.O.P: Choi Yungsuk
— A.Camera: Hwang HoKyu
— Editing: Choi Ida, Moon
   Joonyoung
— Colorist: Han Donggyun
— Sound: Hong Chosun
— Sound recording: Kwak
   Somin
— Scriptor: Kim Minkyung
— Advisor: Im Inja
— Photography: Kim
   Jeongyeop
— Gwangju Coordinator: Do
   Min Ju
— 518 Democratization
   Movement,
— Support by WOW BOOK
   CULTURE & ART
   CENTER, SEO-SeMA
— Production by
   11DANCEPROJECT

그때, 그곳

그때, 그곳

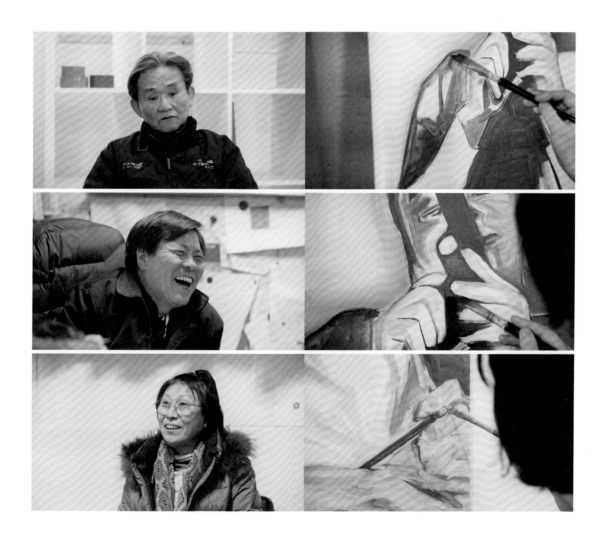

박혜수, ‹기쁜 우리 젊은 날›,
2022, 비디오(강예은 공동연출):
2채널 비디오, 컬러, 사운드,
25분. 작가 소장. 국립현대미술관
지원으로 제작.

Park Hyesoo, *Our Joyful
Young Days*, 2022, video(co-
directed with Kang Yeeun): two-
channel video, color, sound,
25 min. Courtesy of the artist.
Commissioned by MMCA.

그때, 그곳

그때, 그곳

박혜수(함미나), ‹기다리는 남자›,
2022, 캔버스에 유채, 40×40cm.
작가 소장. 국립현대미술관
지원으로 제작.

Park Hyesoo(Ham Mina),
A Waiting Man, 2022, oil on
canvas, 40×40cm. Courtesy of the
artist. Commissioned by MMCA.

박혜수(함미나), ‹울린 남자›,
2022, 나무 판넬에 유채,
53×40.9cm. 작가 소장.
국립현대미술관 지원으로 제작.

Park Hyesoo(Ham Mina),
*The Man Who Made a Woman
Cry*, 2022, oil on wood panel,
53×40.9cm. Courtesy of the artist.
Commissioned by MMCA.

박혜수(함미나), ‹웃는 여자›,
2022, 캔버스에 유채, 27.3×22cm.
작가 소장. 국립현대미술관
지원으로 제작.

Park Hyesoo(Ham Mina),
A Smiling Woman, 2022, oil on
canvas, 27.3×22cm. Courtesy
of the artist. Commissioned
by MMCA.

그때, 그곳

그때, 그곳

뮌, 〈오디토리움(Template
A-Z)〉, 2022, 캐비닛 5개,
오브제, DMX 콘트롤러, 컴퓨터,
모터, 122×50×400cm(5),
700×400×400cm(전체).
작가 소장. 국립현대미술관
지원으로 제작.

Mioon, *Auditorium (Template
A-Z)*, 2022, 5 cabinets, objects,
DMX controlled lights,
motors, 122×50×400cm(5),
700×400×400cm(total). Courtesy
of the artist. Commissioned by
MMCA.

그때, 그곳

143

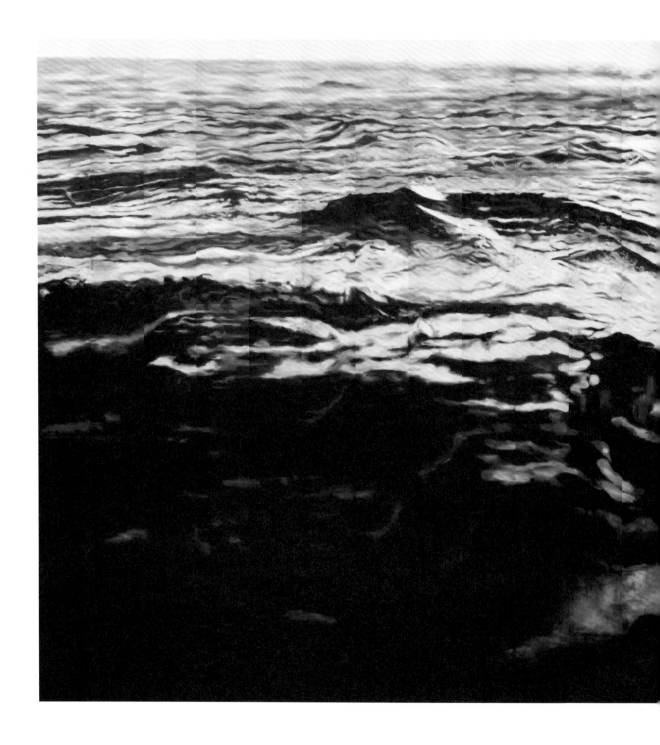

그때, 그곳

홍순명, ‹비스듬한 기억-역설과
연대›, 2022, 캔버스에 유채,
60.5×50cm(240),
605×1,200cm(전체). 작가 소장.
국립현대미술관 지원으로 제작.

Hong Soun, *Oblique Memories–
Irony and Solidarity*, 2022, oil
on canvas, 60.5×50cm(240),
605×1,200cm(total). Courtesy
of the artist. Commissioned by
MMCA.

그때, 그곳

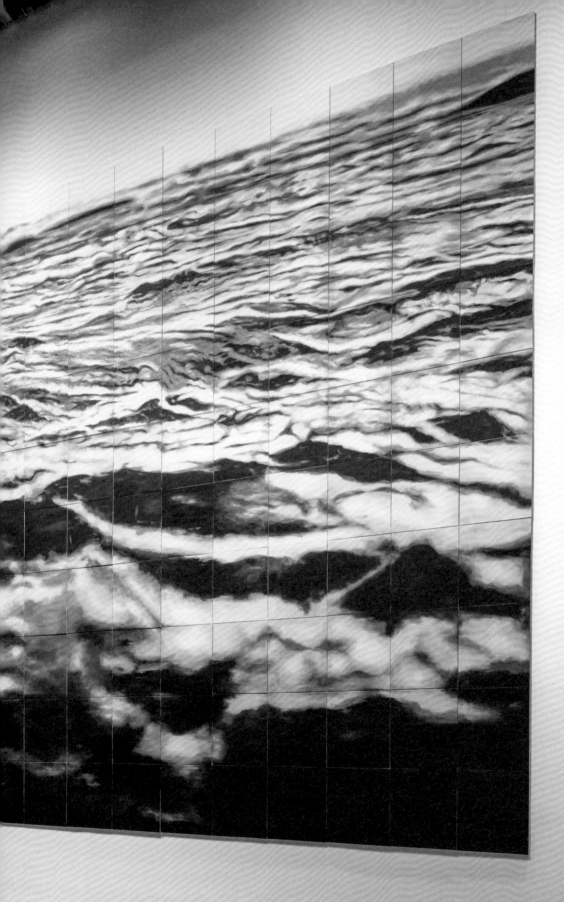

약력　　　　　　　Biography

앤디 워홀(b.1928)
미국 피츠버그 출생,
미국 뉴욕 사망

주요 개인전
2021 《앤디 워홀: 앤디를
찾아서》, 에스파스
루이 비통 서울, 서울
— 《Andy Warhol:
Revelation》,
브루클린뮤지엄,
브루클린, 미국
2020 《Andy Warhol》,
테이트 모던, 런던, 영국
2019 《Andy Warhol: Shadows》,
디아비콘, 뉴욕, 미국
— 《Andy Warhol: From
A to B and Back Again》,
휘트니미술관, 뉴욕, 미국
2018 《Adman: Warhol Before
Pop》, 앤디워홀뮤지엄,
피츠버그, 미국
2017 《Andy Warhol: Dark
Star》, 후멕스 박물관,
멕시코시티, 멕시코
2015 《Andy Warhol:
Campbell's Soup Cans
and Other Works, 1953–
1967》, 뉴욕현대미술관,
뉴욕, 미국

주요 그룹전
2022 《The Dream of the
Museum》, M+, 홍콩
— 《The Whitney's Collection
Selections from 1900 to
1965》, 휘트니미술관,
뉴욕, 미국
2021 《Icons》, 보고시안 재단,
브뤼셀, 벨기에
— 《Wonderland》, 알베르티나
모던, 빈, 오스트리아
2020 《Contemporary Art
Five Propositions》,
보스턴미술관,
보스턴, 미국
2019 《Graphic Revolution
American Prints
1960 to Now》,
세인트루이스 미술관,
세인트루이스, 미국
2018 《MoMA at NGV 130

Years of Modern and
Contemporary Art》,
빅토리아 국립미술관,
멜버른, 호주
2017 《We are here》, 시카고
현대 미술관, 시카고, 미국

주요 소장처
— 앤디워홀뮤지엄,
피츠버그, 미국
— 휘트니미술관, 뉴욕, 미국
— 워커 아트 센터,
미니애폴리스, 미국
— 리움미술관, 서울

허만 콜겐(b.1957)
캐나다 몬트리올 출생,
캐나다 몬트리올 활동

주요 개인전
2021 《Inscape: Voyage to Hidden
Landscape》, 파라다이스
아트스페이스, 인천
2019 《Espage Technologique》,
GTQ, 퀘벡, 캐나다
2017 《Espage Technologique》,
GTQ, 퀘벡, 캐나다
2010 《Ondes: Immanence
Et Matérialité》 AAA,
히슐리유, 캐나다

주요 그룹전
2021 《메타모포시스》,
제5회 국제 디지털
아트 비엔날레,
아스날 컨템포러리 아트,
몬트리올, 캐나다
— 《메타모포시스》, 라이브
시네마 페스티벌 2021,
팔라초 브란카치오,
로마, 이탈리아
2020 《메타모포시스》, 현대
모터스튜디오 서울, 서울
— 《Hexadome》, SXSW 2020,
오스틴, 미국
2019 《Hexadome》,
매사츄세츠 현대미술관,
매사츄세츠, 미국
— 《The Ordinary
Extraordinary》,
SKP 사우스, 베이징, 중국

2016 《Prelude 2016》,
오로라 아트 테크놀로지,
댈러스, 미국
— 《Les Transformables
V.102》, 이스턴 블록,
몬트리올, 캐나다
2014 《다빈치 크리에이티브
2014》, 금천예술공장, 서울
2012 《카타스트로폴로지》,
아르코미술관, 서울

주요 수상
2010 쿼츠 어워드, 파리, 프랑스
2009 쿼츠 어워드, 파리, 프랑스
2004 베스트 독립실험영화
어워드, 뉴욕, 미국

주요 소장처
— 조르주 퐁피두 센터,
파리, 프랑스
— 퀘벡쿠아즈시네마테크,
퀘벡, 캐나다

양정욱(b.1982)
서울 출생, 서울 활동

주요 개인전
2021 《Maybe, It's like that》,
OCI미술관, 서울
2020 《대화의 풍경: 우리는
가끔씩 휘어지던 말을
했다》, 아트벙커, 부천
2019 《어제 찍은 사진을
우리는 잘 보이는
곳에 걸어두었다》,
갤러리현대, 서울
2017 《홀롱, 나는
그것이 필요해요》,
게르게닉미술관,
비냥, 프랑스
2015 《말이 없는 사람》,
두산갤러리, 뉴욕, 미국

주요 그룹전
2021 《상실, 나에게 일어난 모든
일》, 대전시립미술관, 대전
2020 《리듬풍경》, OAG,
오타와, 캐나다
— 《2020 파라다이스
아트랩+》, 파라다이스
아트스페이스, 인천

2019 《가장 멀리서 오는 우리:
도래하는 공동체》,
부산현대미술관, 부산
— 《미술이 사는 그 집》,
FEI 아트 뮤지엄 요코하마,
도쿄, 일본
2018 《별 헤는 날: 나와 당신의
이야기》, 국립현대미술관,
청주
2017 《빈 페이지_Blank Page》,
금호미술관, 서울
2016 《눈 내리는 저녁 숲가에
서서》, 갤러리현대, 서울
2015 《랜덤 액세스》,
백남준아트센터, 용인
2014 《로우테크놀로지:
미래로 돌아가다》,
서울시립미술관, 서울

주요 수상
2020 김세중미술상
청년조각상 수상, 서울
2017 신도 SINAP 작가 선정,
서울

주요 소장처
— 국립현대미술관, 서울
— 서울시립미술관, 서울
— OCI 미술관, 서울
— 유타미술관,
솔트레이크시티, 미국
— 경기도미술관, 안산

임윤경(b.1982)
서울 출생, 서울 활동

주요 개인전
2020 《개인의 자리》,
더레퍼런스, 서울
2016 《친숙한 집단, 낯선 개인》,
스페이스 윌링앤딜링, 서울
2014 《그녀들의 노동》,
175갤러리, 서울

주요 그룹전
2021 《돌봄사회》,
경남도립미술관, 창원
2019 《시간을 보다》,
서울대학교미술관, 서울
— 《번외편: A-side-B》,
금천예술공장 PS333, 서울

Andy Warhol(b.1928)
B. Pittsburgh, U.S.A.,
D. New York, U.S.A.

Selected Solo Exhibitions

2021 *Andy Warhol: Looking for Andy*, Espaces Louis Vitton Seoul, Seoul

— *Andy Warhol: Revelation*, Brooklyn Museum, Brooklyn, U.S.A.

2020 *Andy Warhol*, Tate Modern, London, U.K.

2019 *Andy Warhol: Shadows*, Dia Beacon, New York, U.S.A.

— *Andy Warhol: From A to B and Back Again*, Whitney Museum of American Art, New York, U.S.A.

2018 *Adman: Warhol Before Pop*, The Andy Warhol Musem, Pittsburgh, U.S.A.

2017 *Andy Warhol: Dark Star*, Museo Jumex, Mexico City, Mexico

2015 *Andy Warhol: Campbell's Soup Cans and Other Works, 1953–1967*, Museum of Modern Art, New York, U.S.A.

Selected Group Exhibitions

2022 *The Dream of the Museum*, M+, Hong Kong

— *The Whitney's Collection Selections from 1900 to 1965*, Whitney Museum of American Art, New York, U.S.A.

2021 *Icons*, Boghossian Foundation, Brussels, Belgium

— *Wonderland*, Albertina Modern, Vienna, Austria

2020 *Contemporary Art Five Propositions*, Museum of Fine Arts, Boston, U.S.A.

2019 *Graphic Revolution American Prints 1960 to Now*, Saint Louis Art Musem, Saint Louis, U.S.A.

2018 *MoMA at NGV 130 Years of Modern and Contemporary Art*, National Gallery of Victoria, Melbourne, Australia

2017 *We are here*, Museum of Contemporary Art Chicago, Chicago, U.S.A.

Selected Collections

— The Andy Warhol Musem, Pittsburgh, U.S.A.

— Whitney Museum of American Art, New York, U.S.A.

— Walker Art Center, Minneapolis, U.S.A.

— Leeum Museum of Art, Seoul

Herman Kolgen(b.1957)
Born in Montreal, Canada,
works in Montreal, Canada

Selected Solo Exhibitions

2021 *Inscape: Voyage to Hidden Landscape*, Paradise Art Space, Incheon

2019 *Espage Technologique*, Grand Théâtre de Québec, Québec, Canada

2017 *Expanded Territories*, Fundación Telefónica, Lima, Peru

2010 *Ondes: Immanence Et Matérialité*, Action Art Actuel, Richelieu, Canada

Selected Group Exhibitions

2021 *METAMORPHOSIS*, The 5th International Digital Art Biennial, Arsenal Contemporary Art, Montreal, Canada

— *METAMORPHOSIS*, Live Cinema Festival 2021, Palazzo Brancaccio, Rome, Italy

2020 *METAMORPHOSIS*, Hyundai Motorstudio Seoul, Seoul

— *Hexadome*, SXSW 2020, Austin, U.S.A.

2019 *Hexadome*, Messachusetts Museum of Contemporary Art, Messachusetts, U.S.A.

— *The Ordinary Extraordinary*, SKP South, Beijing, China

2016 *Prelude 2016*, Aurora Art Technology, Dallas, U.S.A.

— *Les Transformables V.102*, Eastern Bloc, Montreal, Canada

2014 *Da Vinci Creative 2014*, Seoul Art Space Geumchoen, Seoul

2012 *Catastrophology*, Arco Art Center, Seoul

Selected Awards

2010 Quartz Award, Paris, France

2009 Quartz Award, Paris, France

2004 Award Best Experimental

Independant Film, New York, U.S.A.

Selected Collections

— Centre Georges Pompidou, Paris, France

— La Cinémathèque québecoise, Montreal, Canada

Yang Junguk(b.1982)
Born in Seoul, works in Seoul

Selected Solo Exhibitions

2021 *Maybe, It's like that*, OCI Museum, Seoul

2020 *Scenery of Dialogue*, Art Bunker, Bucheon

2019 *We Placed the Photograph Taken Yesterday in Plain Sight*, Gallery Hyundai, Seoul

2017 *"Roland, I need it"*, Domaine de Kerguéhennec, Bignan, France

2015 *A Man without Words*, Doosan Gallery, New York, U.S.A.

Selected Group Exhibitions

2021 *Loss, Everything That Happened to Me*, Daejeon Museum of Art, Daejeon

2020 *Rhythm Scape*, OAG, Ottawa, Canada

2020 *Paradise Art Lab+*, Paradise Art Space, Inchon

2019 *Gentil, Gelte: The Advent of a New Community*, Museum of Contemporary Art Busan, Busan

— *That House*, FEI Art Museum Yokohama, Tokyo, Japan

2018 *A Day for Counting Stars: The Story of You & Me*, National Museum of Modern and Contemporary Art, Cheongju

2017 *Blank Page*, Kumho Museum of Art, Seoul

2016 *Stopping by Woods on a Snowy Evening*, Gallery Hyundai, Seoul

2015 *Random Access*, Nam Jun Paik Art Center, Yongin

2014 *Low-Technology: Back to the Future*, Seoul Museum of Art, Seoul

Selected Awards

2020 Kim Se-Choong Sculpture Award, Seoul

2017 Sindoh SINAP, Seoul

Selected Collections

— National Museum of Modern and Contemporary Art, Seoul

— Seoul Museum of Art, Seoul

— OCI Museum, Seoul

— Utah Museum of Fine Arts, Salt Lake City, U.S.A.

— Gyeonggi Museum of Modern Art, Ansan

Lim Yoonkyung(b.1982)
Born in Seoul, works in Seoul

Selected Solo Exhibitions

2020 *One's Position*, The Reference, Seoul

2016 *Familiar Group, Unfamiliar Individual*, Space Willing & Dealing Gallery, Seoul

2014 *Womens' Work*, 175 Gallery, Seoul

Selected Group Exhibitions

2021 *Caring Society*, Gyongnam Art Museum, Changwon

2019 *Seeing Time*, Seoul National University Museum of Art, Seoul

— *Beonwe: A-side-B*, Seoul Art Space Geumcheon PS333, Seoul

2018 *Hidden Workers*, Coreana Museum of Art space*c, Seoul

2017 *Lesson Zero*, National Museum of Modern and Contemporary Art, Gwacheon

2015 *LOVE 1*, Pohang Museum of Steel Art, Pohang

2012 *Whitney Museum Independent Study Program Exhibition*, 161 Bowery, New York, U.S.A.

2010 *S.O.S.*, St. Louis Artists Guild & Galleries, Clayton, U.S.A.

2009 *A Day in the Life: Exploring and Exposing the Everyday*, Kerchhoff Art Gallery, Los Angeles, U.S.A.

Selected Collections

— National Museum of Modern and Contemporary Art, Seoul

Cecilia Vicuña(b.1948)
Born in Santiago, Chile,

2018 «히든 워커스»,
코리아나미술관
스페이스 씨, 서울

2017 «레슨 제로»,
국립현대미술관, 과천

2015 «LOVE 1»,
포항시립미술관, 포항

2012 «휘트니미술관 독립 연구
프로그램 전시», 161
바워리가, 뉴욕

2010 «S.O.S», 세인트 루이스
예술가 길드 & 갤러리,
클레이턴, 미국

2009 «인생에서 하루: 일상의
탐험과 노출», 커프호프
갤러리, 로스앤젤레스, 미국

주요 소장처
— 국립현대미술관, 서울

세실리아 비쿠냐(b.1948)
칠레 산티아고 출생,
미국 뉴욕 및 칠레 산티아고 활동

주요 개인전
2021 «세실리아 비쿠냐:
키푸 기록», 리만머핀, 서울

2019 «Cecilia Vicuña on our
mind», 와티스 인스티튜트,
샌프란시스코, 미국

2018 «Cecilia Vicuña: About to
Happen», 노스마이애미
현대미술관, 마이애미, 미국

2017 «Quipu Desaparecido»,
보스턴미술관, 보스턴, 미국

2010 «Dianna Frid and
Cecilia Vicuña: A Textile
Exhibition», 포이트리
파운데이션, 시카고, 미국

주요 그룹전
2021 «Bodies of Water»,
제13회 상하이비엔날레,
상하이, 중국

— «떠오르는 마음,
맞이하는 영혼»,
제13회 광주비엔날레, 광주

2020 «Witchhunt»,
쿤스탈 샬롯텐보그,
코펜하겐, 덴마크

— «More More More»,

탱크 상하이, 상하이, 중국

2019 «A Year in Art»,
테이트 모던, 런던, 영국

— «Permanent Collection
Rehang», 뉴욕현대미술관,
뉴욕, 미국

2018 «Radical Women: Latin
American Art, 1960-1985»,
브루클린미술관, 브루클린,
미국

2017 «Iterability and Otherness»,
카셀 도큐멘타 14,
카셀, 독일

2016 «A Kingdom of Hours»,
가스웍스, 런던, 영국

2015 «Agitprop!»,
브루클린미술관,
브루클린, 미국

주요 수상
2014 SLAS 봄 2014 스콜라 인
레지던스, 프랫인스티튜트,
뉴욕, 미국

주요 소장처
— 보스턴미술관,
보스턴, 미국
— 구겐하임미술관,
뉴욕, 미국
— 국립미술관,
산티아고, 칠레

시프리앙 가이야르(b.1980)
프랑스 파리 출생,
미국 뉴욕 및 독일 베를린 활동

주요 개인전
2021 «Wolkengarten», 에스파스
루이 비통, 뮌헨, 독일

— «MAM Screen 014:
Cyprien Gaillard»,
모리미술관, 도쿄, 일본

2020 «Nightlife»,
MAC 컨템포러리,
몬트리올, 캐나다

2019 «Ocean II Ocean»,
탱크 상하이, 상하이, 중국

2018 «New Media Series:
Cyprien Gaillard»,
세인트루이스 미술관,
세인트루이스, 미국

주요 그룹전
2021 «Nothing is Lost. Art and
Matter in Transformation»,
GAMec 베르가모,
베르가모, 이탈리아

— «Ambient Temperature»,
후멕스 박물관,
멕시코시티, 멕시코

2019 «May You Live in
Interesting Times»,
제58회 베니스비엔날레,
베니스, 이탈리아

— «Hyper! A Journey
into Art and Sound»,
다이히토어팔렌 함부르크,
함부르크, 독일

2018 «The Polaroid Project.
History of a Medium»,
C/O 베를린, 베를린, 독일

— «Faithless Pictures»,
국립미술관, 오슬로,
노르웨이

2017 «What Absence Is Made
Of», 허쉬혼뮤지엄,
워싱턴 D.C., 미국

— «Material Remain»,
맨체스터예술대학 더
홀든 갤러리, 맨체스터, 영국

2016 «The Infinite Mix: Sound
and Image in Contemporary
Video», 헤이워드 갤러리,
런던, 영국

2015 «City Limit», 더 저널
갤러리, 브루클린, 미국

주요 수상
2016 멜버른 국제 필름 페스티벌
실험영화 단편상,
멜버른, 호주

2012 A.T. 커니 영아티스트
어워드, 뒤셀도르프, 독일

주요 소장처
— 뉴욕현대미술관, 뉴욕, 미국

안리 살라(b.1974)
알바니아 티라나 출생,
독일 베를린 활동

주요 개인전
2019 «AS YOU GO», 카스텔로

디 리볼리, 토리노, 이탈리아

2018 «The Last Resort»,
차고 현대 미술관,
모스코바, 러시아

2017 «Anri Sala», 루피노
타마 요 현대미술관,
멕시코시티, 멕시코

2016 «Anri Sala: Answer Me»,
뉴뮤지엄, 뉴욕, 미국

2015 «The Present Moment»,
하우스 데르 쿤스트,
뮌헨, 독일

주요 그룹전
2020 «모두를 위한 미술관,
개를 위한 미술관»,
국립현대미술관, 서울

— «파도가 지나간 자리»,
서울시립 북서울미술관,
서울

2019 «Intimate distance.
Masterpieces from the
Ishikawa Collection»,
호텔 데 콜렉시옹,
몽펠리에, 프랑스

2018 «Lydia Cabrera and Édouard
Glissant: Trembling
Thinking», 아메리카스
소사이어티, 뉴욕, 미국

— «Take Me (I'm Yours)»,
빌라 메디치, 로마, 이탈리아

2017 «VIVA ARTE VIVA»,
제57회 베니스비엔날레,
베니스, 이탈리아

— «No Place Like Home»,
이스라엘 박물관,
예루살렘, 이스라엘

2016 «L'image volée»,
폰다치오네 프라다,
밀라노, 이탈리아

2015 «Between the Idea and the
Experience», 제15회 아바나
비엔날레, 아바나, 쿠바

2011 «소통의 기술: 안리 살라,
함양아, 필립파레노, 호르헤
파르도», 국립현대미술관,
덕수궁

주요 수상
2014 빈센트 반고흐 비엔날레
어워드 포 컨템포러리
아트 인 유럽, 네덜란드

works in New York, U.S.A.
and Santiago, Chile

Selected Solo Exhibitions

2021 *Cecilia Vicuña: Quipu
Girok*, Lehmann Maupin,
Seoul

2020 *Cecilia Vicuña on our
mind*, The Wattis Institute,
San Francisco, U.S.A.

2019 *Cecilia Vicuña: About
to Happen*, Museum of
Contemporary Art, North
Miami, Miami, U.S.A.

2018 *Quipu Desaparecido*,
Museum of Fine Arts,
Boston, U.S.A.

2017 *Dianna Frid and Cecilia
Vicuña: A Textile
Exhibition*, Poetry
Foundation, Chicago,
U.S.A.

Selected Group Exhibitions

2021 *Bodies of Water*, The 13th
Shangai Biennale, Shangai,
China

— *Minds Rising, Spirits
Tuning*, The 13th Gwangju
Biennale, Gwangju

2020 *Witchhunt*, Kunsthal
Charlottenborg,
Copenhagen, Denmark

— *More More More*, TANK
Shanghai, Shanghai, China

2019 *A Year in Art*, Tate Modern,
London, U.K.

— *Permanent Collection
Rehang*, Museum of
Modern Art, New York,
U.S.A.

2018 *Radical Women: Latin
American Art, 1960–1985*,
Brooklyn Museum,
Brooklyn, U.S.A.

2017 *Iterability and Otherness*,
Documenta 14, Kassel,
Germany

2016 *A Kingdom of Hours*,
Gasworks, London, U.K.

2015 *Agitprop!*, Brooklyn
Museum, Brooklyn, U.S.A.

Selected Awards

2014 SLAS Spring 2014
Scholar in Residence, Pratt
Institute, New York, U.S.A.

Selected Collections

— Museum of Fine Arts,
Boston, U.S.A.

— Solomon R. Guggengeim
Museum, New York,
U.S.A.

— National Museum of Fine

Arts, Santiago, Chile

Cyprien Gaillard(b.1980)
Born in Paris, France,
works in New York, U.S.A.
and Berlin, Germany

Selected Solo Exhibitions

2021 *Wolkengarten*, Espace
Louis Vuitton, Munich,
Germany

— *MAM Screen 014: Cyprien
Gaillard*, Mori Art
Museum, Tokyo, Japan

2020 *Nightlife*, MAC
Contemporary, Montreal,
Canada

2019 *Ocean II Ocean*, TANK
Shanghai, Shanghai, China

2018 *New Media Series: Cyprien
Gaillard*, Saint Louis
Art Musem, Saint Louis,
U.S.A.

Selected Group Exhibitions

2021 *Nothing is Lost. Art and
Matter in Transformation*,
GAMec Bergamo,
Bergamo, Italy

— *Ambient Temperature*,
Museo Jumex, Mexico
City, Mexico

2019 *May You Live in Interesting
Times*, The 58th Venice
Biennale, Venice, Italy

— *Hyper! A Journey into Art
and Sound*, Deichtorhallen
Hamburg, Hamburg,
Germany

2018 *The Polaroid Project.
History of a Medium*, C/O
Berlin, Berlin, Germany

— *Faithless Pictures*, National
Museum, Oslo, Norway

2017 *What Absence Is Made
Of*, Hirshhorn Museum
and Sculpture Garden,
Washington D.C., U.S.A.

— *Material Remain*,
The Holden Gallery,
Manchester School of Art,
Manchester, U.K.

2016 *The Infinite Mix: Sound and
Image in Contemporary
Video*, Hayward Gallery,
London, U.K.

2015 *City Limit*, The Journal
Gallery, Brooklyn, U.S.A.

Selected Awards

2016 Melbourne International
Film Festival Award for
Best Experimental Short
Film, Melbourne, Australia

2012 A.T. Kearney Young
Artist Award, Düsseldorf,
Germany

Selected Collections

— Museum of Modern Art,
New York, U.S.A.

Anri Sala(b.1974)
Born in Tirana, Albania,
works in Berlin, Germany

Selected Solo Exhibitions

2019 *AS YOU GO*, Castello di
Rivoli, Turin, Italy

2018 *The Last Resort*, The
Garage, Moscow, Russia

2017 *Anri Sala*, Museo Tamayo,
Mexico City, Mexico

2016 *Anri Sala: Answer Me*, The
New Museum, New York,
U.S.A.

2015 *The Present Moment*,
Haus der Kunst, Munich,
Germany

Selected Group Exhibitions

2020 *The Museum for All, The
Museum for Dogs*, National
Museum of Modern and
Contemporary Art, Seoul

— *Where the Tide Has Been*,
Buk-Seoul Museum of Art,
Seoul

2019 *Intimate distance.
Masterpieces from the
Ishikawa Collection*,
Hôtel des Collections,
Montpellier, France

2018 *Lydia Cabrera and
Édouard Glissant:
Trembling Thinking*,
Americas Society, New
York, U.S.A.

— *Take Me (I'm Yours)*, Villa
Medici, Rome, Italy

2017 *VIVA ARTE VIVA*, The 57th
Venice Biennale, Venice,
Italy

— *No Place Like Home*,
The Israel Museum,
Jerusalem, Isrel

2016 *L'image volée*, Fondazione
Prada, Milan, Italy

2015 *Between the Idea and the
Experience*, The 15th La
Bienal de La Habana,
Havana, Cuba

2011 *Art of Communication:
Anri Sala, Yang Ah
Ham, Philippe Parreno,
Jorge Pardo*, National
Museum of Modern
and Contemporary Art,

Deoksugung

Selected Awards

2014 Vincent Van Gogh Biennial
Award for Contemporary
Art in Europe, Netherlands

2013 The 10th Benesse Prize,
Okayama, Japan

Selected Collections

— Tate Modern, London, U.K.

— Museum of Contemporary
Art Chicago, Chicago,
U.S.A.

— Centre Georges Pompidou,
Paris, France

Song Joowon(b.1973)
Born in Seoul, works in Seoul

Selected Shows and
Performances

2021 *hwi-i-ing*, SFAC Theater
Quad, Seoul

2020 *Pimple.Blister.Wart.Mole*,
the Former Armed Forces'
Gwangju Hospital

2019 *PungJeong.Gak(風情.刻)
Janganpyeong*,
Janganpyeong Used Car
Market, Seoul

2017 *PungJeong.Gak(風情.刻)
in the Fifth Dimension*,
National Museum of
Modern and Contemporary
Art, Seoul

2016 *PungJeong.Gak(風精.刻)
Nakwon Building*, Nakwon
Instrument Shopping
Center, Seoul

Solo Exhibitions

2019 *As reflection does not
reflect on its own reflection*,
Incheon Art Platform,
Incheon

2018 *Pungjeong.Gak 1–8*, d/p,
Seoul

Selected Group Exhibitions
and Screening

2022 *To you: Move Toward
Where You Are*, ARKO Art
Center, Seoul

2021 London International
Screen Dance Festival,
London, U.K.

— *Signaling Perimeters*,
Nam-Seoul Museum of Art,
Seoul

— *Solid City*, Sewha Museum
of Art, Seoul

2020 Dance Camera West Film
Festival, Los Angeles,

U.S.A

— *Ex-Cinema: A Movie outside the Movie*, Seoul Art Cinema, Seoul
— The 20th Seoul Independent Documentary Film Festival, Seoul
— *16 Columns: A roofless gallery-PS333*, Seoul Art Space Geumcheon, Seoul
2019 The 45th Seoul Independent Film Festival, Seoul
— The 21st Seoul International Women's Film Festival, Seoul

Selected Awards
2021 FuoriFormato Film Festival, Audience Award, Genoa, Italy
2020 Minister of Culture, Sports and Tourism's Citation, Seoul
2018 The 18th Seoul International New Media Festival, Audience Jury Award, Seoul
2017 Korea Dance Critics Awards, Best Prize, Seoul
— The 1st Seoul Dance Film Festival, Best Film Prize, Seoul

Akram Zataari(b.1966)
Born in Sidon, Lebanon, works in Beirut, Lebanon

Selected Solo Exhibitions
2019 *Against Photography*, Sharjah Art Foundation, Sharjah, U.A.E.
2018 *Against Photography*, National Museum of Modern and Contemporary Art, Seoul
2017 *Against Photography*, Barcelona Museum of Contemporary Art, Barcelona, Spain
2016 *Letter to a Refusing Pilot*, Thomas Dane Gallery, London, U.K.
2015 *Akram Zaatari*, SALT, Istanbul, Turkey

Selected Group Exhibitions
2021 *Unsettled Objects*, Sharjah Art Foundation, Sharjah, U.A.E.
2020 *Masculinities. Liberation through Photography*, Barbican Centre, London, U.K.

2019 *BEYOND: Modern and Contemporary Lebanese Art and Design*, Phillips, London, U.K.
— *Making New Time*, Sharjah Art Foundation, Sharjah, U.A.E.
2018 *Swingers*, Greene Naftali Gallery, New York, U.S.A.
— *En Rebeldía (In Rebellion)*, Valencia Museum of Modern Art, Valencia, Spain
2017 *Home Beirut. Sounding the Neighbours*, MAXXI, Rome, Italy
— *ISelf Collection: The End of Love*, Whitechapel Gallery, London, U.K.
2016 *Question the Wall Itself*, Walker Art Center, Minneapolis, U.S.A.
2015 *Arte Fiera Collezionismi– Too Early Too Late. Middle East and Modernity*, Pinacoteca Nazionale di Bologna, Bologna, Italy

Selected Awards
2011 Yanghyun Prize, Seoul

Selected Collections
— Centre Georges Pompidou, Paris, France
— Solomon R. Guggengeim Museum, New York, U.S.A.
— Tate Modern, London, U.K.

Louise Bourgeois(b.1911)
B. Paris, France,
D. New York, U.S.A.

Selected Solo Exhibitions
2022 *Louise Bourgeois: Paintings*, The Metropolitan Museum of Art, New York, U.S.A.
— *Louise Bourgeois. The Woven Child*, Martin-Gropius-Bau, Berlin, Germany
2021 *The Smell of Eucalyptus*, Kukje Gallery, Seoul
— *Maladie de l'Amour*, Hauser & Wirth, Monaco, Monaco
— *Louise Bourgeois: Freud's Daughter*, The Jewish Museum, New York, U.S.A.

Selected Group Exhibitions
2022 *Louise Bourgeois x Jenny*

Holzer. The Violence of Handwriting Across a Page, Kunstmuseum Basel, Basel, Switzerland
— *girls girls girls*, Lismore Castle Arts, Lismore, Ireland
— *A Century of the Artist's Studio: 1920–2020*, Whitechapel Gallery, London, U.K.
2021 *Human, Seven Questions*, Leeum Museum of Art, Seoul
— *Body Topographies*, Lehmann Maupin, London, U.K.
— *Le Surréalisme dans l'art américain*, Centre de la vieille Charité–Ville de Marseille, Marseille, France
— *Mother!*, Kunsthalle Mannheim, Mannheim, Germany
2020 *i'm yours: Encounters with Art in Our Times*, The Institute of Contemporary Art, Boston, U.S.A.
— *Fantastic Women. Surrel Worlds From Meret Oppenheim to Louise Bourgeois*, Louisiana Museum of Modern Art, Humlebaek, Denmark
2019 *Beyond Infinity. Contemporary Art After Kusama*, The Institute of Contemporary Art, Boston, U.S.A.

Selected Collections
— Museum of Modern Art, New York, U.S.A.
— Solomon R. Guggengeim Museum, New York, U.S.A.
— Tate, London, U.K.

Park Hyesoo(b.1974)
Born in Seoul, works in Seoul

Selected Solo Exhibitions
2021 *Come Closer, But Not That Close*, Kyobo Art Space, Seoul
2018 *Community Platform 3377*, Shinheungdong Public Art Gallery, Seongnam
2017 *Nowhere Man*, This Weekend Room, Seoul
2016 *Now Here is Nowhere*, SongEun Art Space, Seoul

Selected Group Exhibitions
2021 *The Nature of Art*, Busan Museum of Art, Busan
— *TRAUMA: 15 MINUTES*, Daejeon Museum of Art, Daejeon
2020 *The Better Man 1948-2020: Pick your representative for the National Assembly*, Ilmin Museum of Art, Seoul
— *Reality Error*, Nam June Pait Art Center, Yongin
2019 *Korea Artist Prize 2019*, National Museum of Modern and Contemporary Art, Seoul
— *The Phenomenon of the Mind: Facing Yourself*, Museum of Contemporary Art Busan, Busan
2018 *Re: Sense*, Coreana Museum of Art, Seoul
— *Hard Boiled and Toxic*, Gyeonggi Museum of Modern Art, Ansan
2017 *Do It Seoul*, Ilmin Museum of Art, Seoul
2016 *Somewhere @ Nowhere*, Seoul Olympic Museum of Art, Seoul
2015 *APMAP-Researcher's Way*, Amorepacific Museum of Art, Yongin
2014 *Future is Now*, MAXXI, Rome, Italy

Selected Awards
2014 The 13th SongEun Arts Award, Grand Prize, SongEun Art Foundation, Seoul

Selected Collections
— National Museum of Modern and Contemporary Art, Seoul
— Seoul Museum of Art, Seoul
— Museum of Contemporary of Art Busan, Busan

Mioon
Kim Minsun(b. 1972)
Born in Seoul, works in Seoul
Choi Moonsun(b. 1972)
Born in Seoul, works in Seoul

Selected Solo Exhibitions
2017 *Unfinished Relay*, Arco Art Center, Seoul
2016 *MIOON ZIP: Oh, My Public*, Paradise ZIP, Seoul
2014 *Memory Theater*, Coreana

박혜수(b.1974)
서울 출생, 서울 활동

주요 개인전
2021 «가까이, 조금 멀리
있어줘», 교보아트
스페이스, 서울
2018 «커뮤니티 플랫폼 3377»,
신흥창작소갤러리, 성남
2017 «Nowhere Man»,
디스위켄드룸, 서울
2016 «Now Here is Nowhere»,
송은아트스페이스, 서울

주요 그룹전
2021 «이토록 아름다운»,
부산시립미술관, 부산
— «트라우마: 퓰리처상
사진전&15분»,
대전시립미술관, 대전
2020 «새일꾼 1948-2020:
여러분의 대표를 뽑아
국회로 보내시오»,
일민미술관, 서울
— «현실이상»,
백남준아트센터, 용인
2019 «올해의작가상 2019»,
국립현대미술관, 서울
— «마음현상:
나와 마주하기»,
부산현대미술관, 부산
2018 «Re: Sense»,
코리아나미술관, 서울
— «Hard Boiled and Toxic»,
경기도미술관, 안산
2017 «Do It Seoul»,
일민미술관, 서울
2016 «어느 곳도 아닌 이곳»,
소마미술관, 서울
2015 «APMAP-연구자의 길»,
아모레퍼시픽미술관, 용인
2014 «미래는 지금이다»,
로마 국립현대미술관,
로마, 이탈리아

주요 수상
2014 제13회 송은 미술대상전
대상, 송은문화재단, 서울

주요 소장처
— 국립현대미술관, 서울
— 서울시립미술관, 서울

— 부산현대미술관, 부산

뮌
김민선(b. 1972)
서울 출생, 서울 활동
최문선(b. 1972)
서울 출생, 서울 활동

주요 개인전
2017 «미완의 릴레이»,
아르코미술관, 서울
2016 «MIOON ZIP:
Oh, My Public»,
파라다이스 ZIP, 서울
2014 «기억극장»,
코리아나미술관
스페이스 씨, 서울
2013 «Kaleidoscope»,
스페이스캔, 베이징, 중국

주요 그룹전
2022 «찬란한 날들»,
울산시립미술관, 울산
— «나를 만나는 계절»,
대구미술관, 대구
2020 «1920 기억극장:
황금광시대»,
일민미술관, 서울
— «별이 된 사람들»,
광주시립미술관, 광주
2019 «웹-레트로», 서울시립
북서울미술관, 서울
— «공공미술전 2015-
2018: 함께 할래»,
경기도미술관, 안산
2018 «미래를 걷는 사람들»,
부산현대미술관, 부산
— «몸소전»,
우란문화재단, 서울
2016 «불확실성, 연결과-공존»,
수원시립아이파크미술관,
수원
2015 «수퍼전파:
미디어 바이러스»,
백남준아트센터, 용인
2014 «공간의 기억»,
문화역서울 284, 서울

주요 수상
2021 박동준상(미술부문),
박동준기념사업회, 대구

2009 제9회 송은미술대상 대상,
송은문화재단, 서울
2005 젊은 예술가상
(미디어아트),
노르트라인베스트팔렌
(NRW) 주정부, 독일

주요 소장처
— 국립현대미술관, 서울
— 서울시립미술관, 서울
— 부산시립미술관, 부산

홍순명(b.1959)
서울 출생, 서울 활동

주요 개인전
2020 «흔한 믿음, 익숙한 오해»,
조현화랑, 부산
2019 «Sidescape-Objection»,
1335 마비니 갤러리,
마닐라, 필리핀
2018 «X의, Y의, 그리고 Z의»,
아마도예술공간, 서울
2017 «홍순명: 장밋빛 인생»,
대구미술관, 대구
2016 «제1회 전혁림미술상
수상작가 초대전»,
전혁림미술관, 통영

주요 그룹전
2021 «DMZ 아트&피스
플랫폼», 유니마루, DMZ
2020 «작업-판데믹의
한 가운데서
예술의 길을 묻다»,
서울대학교미술관, 서울
2019 «DMZ»,
문화역서울284, 서울
— «인왕산 아회첩-유서산기»,
보안여관, 서울
2018 «보이스리스»,
서울시립미술관, 서울
— «균열 Ⅱ»,
국립현대미술관, 과천
2017 «망각에 부치는 노래»,
서울시립 남서울미술관,
서울
2016 «4월의 동행»,
경기도미술관, 안산
2015 «나-잠시만 눈을
감아보세요»,

마라야 아트센터, 샤르자,
아랍에미레이트
— «플라스틱 신화»,
국립아시아문화전당, 광주

주요 수상
2016 제17회 이인성미술상,
대구미술관, 대구
2015 제1회 전력림미술상,
전력림미술관, 통영

주요 소장처
— 국립현대미술관, 서울
— 서울시립미술관, 서울
— 경기도미술관, 안산
— 파리국립미술학교, 파리,
프랑스

Museum of Art space*c,
Seoul

2013 *Kaleidoscope*, Space CAN,
Beijing, China

Selected Group Exhibitions
2022 *The Brilliant Day*, Ulsan
Art Museum, Ulsan
— *A Season of Meditation*,
Daegu Art Museum, Daegu
2020 *1920 Memory Theater: The
Gold Rush*, Ilmin Museum
of Art, Seoul
— *To Reach Star*, Gwangju
Museum of Art, Gwangju
2019 *WEB-RETRO*, Buk-Seoul
Museum of Art, Seoul
— *Public Art Project 2015–
2018: With, Together*,
Gyeonggi Museum of
Modern Art, Ansan
2018 *People Walking the Future*,
Museum of Contemporary
Art Busan, Busan
— *PERSONALLY*, Wooran
Foundation, Seoul
2016 *Uncertainty, Connection
and Coexistence*, Suwon
Museum of Art, Suwon
2015 *Super-spreader: Media
Virus*, Nam Jun Paik Art
Center, Yongin
2014 *Memory of Space*, Culture
Station Seoul 284, Seoul

Selected Awards
2021 Pakdongjun Prize(Visual
Arts), P.D.J Memorial
Foundation, Daegu
2009 The 9th SongEun Arts
Award, Grand Prize,
SongEun Art Foundation,
Seoul
2005 Award for young
artists(Media art), State
Parliament of North Rhine-
Westphalia, Germany

Selected Collections
— National Museum of
Modern and Contemporary
Art, Seoul
— Seoul Museum of Art,
Seoul
— Busan Museum of Art,
Busan

Hong Soun(b.1959)
Born in Seoul, works in Seoul

Selected Solo Exhibitions
2020 *Typical belief, Typical
misconception*, Johyun
Gallery, Busan

2019 *Sidescape-Objection*, 1335
Mabini Gallery, Manila,
Philippines
2018 *of the X, Y, and Z*, Amado
Art Space/Lab, Seoul
2017 *Hong Soun: La vie en rose*,
Daegu Art Museum, Daegu
2016 *Price of Jeon Hyuk Lim*,
Jeon Hyuk Lim Art
Museum, Tongyeong

Selected Group Exhibitions
2021 *DMZ Art&Peace Platform*,
UniMARU, DMZ
2020 *Art Work: Seeking Passage
of Art Upon Pandemic*,
Seoul National University
Museum of Art, Seoul
2019 *DMZ*, Culture Station
Seoul 284, Seoul
— *Inwangsan Project*,
Artspace BOAN, Seoul
2018 *Voiceless*, Seoul Museum
of Art, Seoul
— *Cracks in the Concrete II*,
Museum of Modern
and Contemporary Art,
Gwacheon
2017 *Ode à l'oubli*, Nam-Seoul
Museum of Art, Seoul
2016 *MV Seoul Memorial
Exhibition: April the
Eternal Voyage*, Gyeonggi
Museum of Modern Art,
Ansan
2015 *[ana] please keep your
eyes closed for a moment*,
Maraya Art Centre,
Sharjah, U.A.E.
— *Plastic Myth*, Asia Culture
Center, Gwangju

Selected Awards
2016 The 17th The
LEEINSUNG Art Prize,
Daegu Art Museum, Daegu
2015 The 1st Jeon Hyuk Lim
Art Award, Jeon Hyuk Lim
Museum of Art, Tongyeong

Selected Collections
— National Museum of
Modern and Contemporary
Art, Seoul
— Seoul Museum of Art,
Seoul
— Gyeonggi Museum of
Modern Art, Ansan
— École des Beaux-Arts,
Paris, France

전시

기간
2022년 4월 8일-8월 7일

장소
국립현대미술관
서울 5전시실

주최
국립현대미술관

관장
윤범모

학예연구실장
김준기

현대미술1과장
류지연

학예연구관
박수진

전시기획
김은주

전시진행
정해선, 유채린

전시디자인
김소희

그래픽디자인
허은지

공간조성
윤해리, 김정은

운송·설치
정재환, 주창하, 추현지

작품보존
범대건, 이남이, 조인애,
윤보경, 한예빈, 최윤정,
최양호

홍보·마케팅
이성희, 윤승연, 박유리,
채지연, 김홍조, 김민주
이민지, 기성미, 신나래,
장라윤, 김보윤

교육
윤지영, 조정원, 황호경

고객지원
이은수, 주다란, 황보경

사진
홍철기

출판

발행인
윤범모

편집인
김준기

제작총괄
류지연, 박수진

편집
김은주

편집지원
정해선, 유채린

교정·교열
권태현

번역
콜린 모엣, 박명숙

디자인
리센트워크

인쇄·제본
으뜸프로세스

초판 발행
2022년 4월 30일

발행처
국립현대미술관,
서울시 종로구 삼청로 30
02 3701 9500
mmca.go.kr

ISBN 978-89-6303-308-2
값 25,000원

감사의 말씀
글래드스톤갤러리, 리만머핀, 마리안굿맨갤러리,
샹탈크루젤갤러리, 앤디워홀뮤지엄, 토마스데인갤러리,
파라다이스 아트스페이스 그리고 전시를 도와주신 많은 분들께
진심으로 감사의 말씀을 드립니다.

Exhibition

Period
8 April–7 August, 2022

Venue
National Museum of Modern
and Contemporary Art, Seoul,
Gallery 5

Organized by
National Museum of Modern
and Contemporary Art, Korea

Director
Youn Bummo

Chief Curator
Gim Jungi

Head of Exhibition
Department 1
Liu Jienne

Senior Curator
Park Soojin

Curator
Kim Eunju

Curatorial Assistant
Chung Haesun, Yoo Chaerin

Exhibition Design
Kim Sohee

Graphic Design
Heo Eunji

Space Construction
Yun Haeri, Kim Jungeun

Technical Coordination
Jeong Jaewhan, Ju Changha,
Choo Hyunji

Conservation
Beom Daegon, Lee Nami,
Cho Inae, Yoon Bokyung,
Han Yebin, Choi Yoonjeong,
Choi Yangho

Public Relations and Marketing
Lee Sunghee, Yun Tiffany,
Park Yuree, Chae Jiyeon,
Kim Hongjo, Kim Minjoo,
Lee Minjee, Ki Sungmi,
Shin Narae, Jang Layoon,
Kim Boyoon

Education
Yoon Jeeyoung, Cho Jeongwon,
Hwang Hokyung

Customer Service
Lee Eunsu, Ju Daran,
Hwang Bokyung

Photography
Hong Cheolki

Publication

Publisher
Youn Bummo

Production director
Gim Jungi

Managed by
Liu Jienne, Park Soojin

Edited by
Kim Eunju

Sub-edited by
Chung Haesun, Yoo Chaerin

Revision
Kwon Taehyun

Translation
Colin Mouat, Park Myoungsook

Design
RecentWork

Printing and Binding
Top Process Cp., Ltd

First Publishing Date
30 April 2022

Published by
National Museum of Modern
and Contemporary Art, Korea
30 Samcheong-ro, Jongno-gu,
Seoul, Republic of Korea
02 3701 9500
mmca.go.kr

ISBN 978-89-6303-308-2
KRW 25,000

Acknowledgements
The MMCA would like to express our sincere thanks to Gladstone
Gallery, Lehmann Maupin, Marian Goodman Gallery, Galerie Chantal
Crousel, The Andy Warhol Museum, Thomas Dane Gallery, Paradise Art
Space, and all of whom supported this exhibition.